# MERLYN'S MEMOIRS

## ENGLISH SPRINGER SPANIEL EXTRAORDINAIRE

### BY

# MERLYN

## TRANSLATED BY Jo Meintjes

**TSL Publications**

First published in Great Britain in 2019
By TSL Publications, Rickmansworth

Copyright © 2019 Jo Meintjes

ISBN / 978-1-913294-14-4

**Dedicated to Jo's cousin
John Woodcock**

former cricket correspondent of *The Times*
and former editor of *Wisden*

and erstwhile owner of English Springer Spaniels:
Flight, Googly, Gully, Long Stop, Slip, Spinner,
Stumper and Yorker
many of whom Jo knew where she grew up in Longparish,
Hampshire

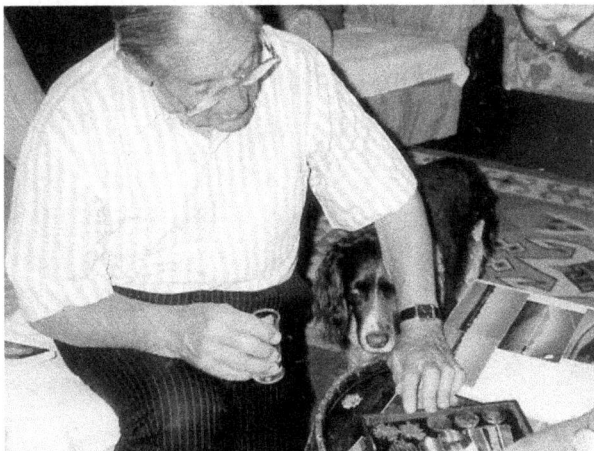

*I am looking at Dad's family Boer War medals with Mum's
cousin John Woodcock (the Times Cricket Correspondent in the
UK) who came for dinner of Springbok which Dad had hunted.
This was in December 1994 to report on the English (who were
losing vs the South African, Springbok, cricket team).*

# FOREWOOF

I am Merlyn, a liver and white English Springer Spaniel. All these stories are true.

Although you may think I was satisfying my own needs (yes I probably was) I felt I trod a new path with my exploits and crossed new boundaries. This is how dogs and humans (in that order) should live their lives.

Fortunately my Mum, Jo, helped put my paw to these memoirs – it's high time too as I lived as I did on earth from November 1983 to May 2000 but I never got any older or thought I couldn't attempt something unusual like climbing to the top of the 2m high outside toilet.

Springers unite – we are an exceptionally special breed and can teach humans a thing or three. Mum should know, she has homed (we don't say owned) many Springers since me in the early 1980s to the present.

I hope this book will help you live *your* life as *you* wish.

*Little young me. I don't like being paraded around!*

# INTRODUCTION

I didn't want to go home with them. A man and a woman came to visit me soon after I appeared on this earth. I was quite happy where I was with my dog Mum called Abigail and a few others like me. This couple came again and said "Happy Christmas" or some weird greeting. I really showed my objection at being cuddled by pooping on the lady's skirt.

I was then bundled off unceremoniously in early January in a car and carried inside a house to find a lot of furniture all over the place. I heard them say "the move went well but we are exhausted" to friends who came over with some supper. I hoped I was getting some – oh just biscuits with some gravy and meat from a tin for me. That night I was barricaded in the kitchen so I squealed a lot. How *could* they leave me all by myself?!!

We all endured my tuneful renditions for about three nights before I gained entry to the bedroom.

But not before I had a surprise for my Dad, Chris. I found a veggie rack filled with boring potatoes and onions. But here was a bulb of something tasty. I ate the lot. When Mum Jo opened the kitchen door I ran into the bedroom instead of being "a good boy" outside. I stood on Dad's chest and breathed heavily after my exertions. "Oh no" the inert creature said and a few rude words followed. I was quite shocked to be greeted like that.

After all I was an adorable pup with my brown and white markings and blue eyes which you get given until about three months of age when they turn an irresistible liquid brown. I had eaten a whole bulb of garlic, not just a clove or two. That was a Sunday to remember as Mum sets down my memoirs some 34 years later.

I have something to say about that from my cloud – "About time too". No other English Springer Spaniel – and I understand Mum Jo has the 11th, 12th and 13th Springer since *moi* as we write this in 2019 – has had a life quite like mine.

I had to learn that when they called Merlyn, that was my cue to appear; but I was usually far too busy with my own agenda. They really had a nerve.

Ah well, what it is to have my say post mortem . . .

*Lessons for Humans*

1. Don't assume I want to live with *you.* Puppyhood with my siblings and Mum is just fine thank you.
2. Do not leave me on my own when I am so little.
3. Give me enough to eat, garlic is fine for starters.

*Happier times with my trainer Lionel as he had now emigrated back to England. After ten years he visited us during Easter – see the Easter Egg story.*

# EASTER SUNDAY 1996

My folks decided to have some people round, including Lionel, who had once owned my Mum, Abigail, and had travelled over the ocean having given up training dogs in South Africa.

He brought some family with him including small children plus a couple of other entertaining radio people as my folk were often interviewed on the radio. Mum devised a contest. There would be four teams. Each person would run from their chair to pick up a lead, attach it to the dog (chosen by lucky draw from a hat) and rush into the garden to find as many Easter eggs as possible. Apparently they used to run to their cars at the start of Grand Prixs. Instead of cars, it was dogs. This sounded like fun.

There were four participants on my side as by now I had a wife, Robyn, daughter Kerry, and the stray, but Springer Holly, who arrived as a few weeks old pup but was now four years old.

I kept watch over the back garden, the scene of the action, out of the kitchen window as I was rather partial to chocolate which never did me any harm. I could see Lionel's grandson had the same idea. We could see where Mum hid these tasty morsels.

Why bother sniffing when you can see where to look with your eyes? I sat on a chair to do this as the windows were above the sink. It was no problem to jump onto a chair, as to keep myself amused when I was a pup I ran at full tilt down the small Parkhurst garden to perch on the boundary wall.

There at least I could see more of the world, mainly the neighbour's veggie garden below me.

Once I made a mistake when my parents were gadding on a trip. House sitter, Melanie, couldn't find me anywhere. It was long before these days of easy texting overseas to see if Mum and Dad had any ideas where I could hide.

Maybe a neighbour gave a clue saying I was used to sitting on the wall. Oh yes, it was probably that neighbour Anne. She got very cross with my parents that I sat on a wall as her "Boot", the large fluffy cat, also had the idea that walls were his territory. So we would meet at the cross roads of where the walls joined. Boot nearly had a heart attack as did his owner crying plaintively "Bo-oo-oot" in several rising octaves, "Where are you? B-o-oo-t! Come to Mummy. Your din-dins is served!"

Melanie walked round the block to ring the neighbour's bell: "Have you seen a small brown and white dog?" she asked almost in tears. The Italian gent replied not speaking ze Engleesh, "No, no dog here." Eventually she prevailed and the Italian and her found me crouching in his runner beans. And he was suitably furious! As it was quite a drop on his side of the wall I could not take a running jump to return the way I had come. Anyway there were far too many obstacles like cabbages in the way. I was quite relieved as by now it was my dinner time.

Sadly that put a stop to my efforts as he was a spoil-sport and put up some barbed wire.

However back to my reminiscing: I drew the name of some slow female as a partner so I was eliminated from this contest after the two teams played each other much to my annoyance.

My daughter Kerry and Holly were in the finals. Robyn was not in the least competitive, more about her in another story. Kerry won the contest as the little kid stuffed all the eggs in his upturned tee-shirt to form a pouch, but somehow kept hold of Kerry's lead, who was a "goodie-goodie" anyway and wouldn't have pulled to hurry her partner along, as I would have, of course.

It was such a fun day, lunch only finished at 6 p.m. – as Dad made these endless venison *potjies** which cooked slowly so we only ate late. We'd "found" this meat on our hunting trips. Sadly I didn't have too much success in that department either.

*Lessons for Humans*
1. If you must arrange games, expect me to cheat.
2. Put walls around your garden and I will leap onto them or sometimes over.

*Me climbing the wall at the end of our garden.*

---

* a *potjie* is a meat dish cooked over an open fire in a tri-legged pot, almost as popular in South Africa as the *braai*, sorry barbecue.

# HUNTING ... WELL SORT OF

Apparently my abilities were not top rated. I can't think why. When I was barely more than a pup Dad said I must go and help him. Ooh, I was always ready for that, in the *bakkie* (*a pick up for non South Africans*) I sprang as a good Springer should. We drove and drove and I was starting to need a wee. I hadn't learned to lift my leg yet. When I did, this caused much excitement to be told elsewhere. But more excitement was at paw than having a squat when I arrived. There were lots of birds pecking at the ground and clucking away at each other. So here I was "to the rescue". I could easily get one for Dad and our hunting would be done for the day.

Off the *bakkie* I leapt before Dad had even time to say "*Goeie môre*" to the farmer and within a blink of an eye, I had nailed one of these clucking devils. Ooops apparently this was not wanted – much bowing and scraping followed in Afrikaans, a language I hadn't yet mastered, but Dad could speak fluently, unlike Mum. English commands were bad enough. I was in the dog house – apparently not a nice place to be.

The farmer had to eat compulsory chicken for Sunday lunch that weekend. I was told I was lucky not to be shot at dawn!

I was quite useful another time running after an injured warthog and letting Dad finish it off. But soon I was happy in later life to hand the baton to my daughter Kerry who was exemplary. I think that means well-behaved.

She curled up on Dad's camp bed for a good snooze after some kilometres were walked early one morning. Dad lit a *braai;* put on the sausages and steak for a good brunch when his pal Klaus re-appeared. While all was sizzling Dad needed a bathroom break so off he went.

When he came back to turn the food over there was none. He was extremely puzzled: had he put the food on? Where was it? Kerry was in her same position sleeping but there may have been a slight smile on her face as Springers do smile when they are content and their tums are full.

Just at that moment Klaus appeared in camp. He was not amused to find no food to eat.

*Lessons for Humans*

1. Birds are for chasing. A chicken is a bird in my dictionary.
2. Don't leave food around even on the barbecue

Just one more "tail" to tell in this department – 'cos I thought I was exemplary here! Dad, Mum, my new girlfriend Robyn and *moi* set off to a farm south of Jo'burg where there was to be a shoot. Now that I have learnt about eco things it was most unfair. The pheasants were kept in fairly large cages and only released that morning. In fact, some were put in fairly small cages and put high up in trees. The guys could release them by opening the hatches and out they would flutter, usually to the ground. This is where they needed me and Robyn.

But it was a cold winter's morning and Robyn had slunk off somewhere. She was so gentle it was amazing, she had had lots of litters of pups who became gun dogs. I should explain she was previously owned by Lionel, my breeder and trainer. He was imminently departing for the UK so this glamorous lady with a pedigree as long as your arm, was bequeathed to us.

In fact her pedigree could be said to be royal! Her family line was among the Springers bred on Sandringham Estate, belonging to Her Majesty, The Queen of England. Mum found this out later by mentioning her breeding in a Christmas card to Cousin Michael who bred horses there for the Queen Mother. Years later, on a cold May morning they visited the royal kennels.

Back to this winter day – so this was all up to me to make these darn birds fly again if I couldn't catch them like the chickens. Springers can run right, then left, a manoeuvre known as "quartering". If there is a handy pond and the bird falls in then we dive in! No worries, us lot can take care of everything, unlike some of those slow but handsome Labradors, Retrievers and the like. So I was really energetic but mustn't go too far ahead of those humans with shotguns as it wasn't a proper organised affair like Mum had been on as a handler with her Dad, a keen shot, with his fancy Purdey gun nearly being pulled flat into the Hampshire ploughed mud as one of the family Labs was so eager to help. Her own Mother had long given up such strenuous exercise.

There is a famous photo of me looking in the opposite direction behind Dad when most gundogs would be sitting looking forward. Well, I was only watching his back as would have been appreciated in this day and age with all the baddies creeping around. We soon had a tidy pile of these poor dead birds and were told to divide up the spoils. Mum was horrified: in England each "gun", i.e. people like her Dad, would be handed a brace (two) of pheasants to take home for the pot.

The only problem remaining now was what had happened to Robyn? She had once lived nearby so knew the farm well. It didn't take long to find her curled up by a roaring log fire.

We all warmed ourselves and the humans ate some tasty sandwiches and had drinks; I was given a decent hand-out and found a bowl of fresh water. A quick zizz and I was ready to start all over again.

Sadly, it appeared that it was all done and dusted for the day.

*Lessons for Humans*
1. Springers are very helpful souls and in this case I was actually rewarded.
2. I guarded Dad's rear – just in case some critter, human or otherwise crept up on him.
3. If you don't like loud bangs go and make yourself comfortable elsewhere.

# STATIONARY ANIMAL?

When I was taken to the conservation society – where Mum worked – as a pup, I saw this big animal with graceful curving horns, which I learned was a Sable Antelope (the logo of the society), standing in their entrance hall.

The society had this animal as its mascot. It was a bit scary for me; I growled, but eventually I plucked up courage to sniff it. Oh fine, it wasn't alive but just to show my bravery I marked it by lifting my leg. I wasn't to know these were their new offices and a brand new carpet had just been put down a few days earlier.

*Lesson for Humans*

1. I was only marking the territory for Springers before someone else claimed it.

*My very pedigreed 'wife' Robyn.*

# MY GROWING FAMILY

Although I thought Robyn was great and had met her several times at Lionel's, I was pretty horrified when she arrived in May 1985 with six pups in tow. Not mine I hasten to add! That really is taking liberties I am sure you will agree?

Our garden was only small as we lived in Parkhurst, otherwise known as Barkhurst, the whole area with house took up an area of less than 500 m². So I had to side-step these little horrors. Ankle-biters was too kind a word for them. At that age they have needle-sharp teeth aiming for my appendage thinking it was a milk bar (their Mum's teat).

No wonder my real Mum, Abigail, nor my Human Mum thanked me for sinking my tiny teeth in their flesh when I was small. It was my turn to hop, skip and jump out of the way.

Fortunately Robyn had done all this mothering business many times before and soon they were ready to be packed off to their new owners.

The reason for this apparently was we all had visited them on this small-holding south of Jo'burg where Lionel didn't have a phone (and it was long before cell/mobile phones were thought of) so how were potential buyers of the pups going to visit and give them new homes? Chris and Jo saw no problem fielding the phone calls and making appointments.

They owed Lionel a favour as when they visited, someone left the gate open and all the adult dogs went off for an excursion. It was black-jack time and they came back covered in them and happily left Lionel to deal with tidying the dogs up. Black-jacks are nasty seeds of a plant from South America which the English brought in with their hay to feed their horses in the Anglo-Boer War conflict (now called the South African War). The black-jacks happily made their home here. They are really spiky and can even stick to human skin.

Mum Jo was off to a function in Durban and thought nothing of putting two pups in a cardboard box to deliver one to Durban and the other to Umkomaas on the South Coast. Just as she left Jo'burg there was a road where they have a short 60 km/hr speed limit on a single lane.

The police often catch you there for speeding, which they did. Luckily the contents of the cardboard box on the back seat remained quiet. Mum didn't know it's illegal to take pups from one province to the other without their rabies jabs which of course they were too young to have. They would have had some immunity from Robyn's milk. Apparently it's no good hurrying things up and giving them the rabies jabs too early as it's a waste of time and rejected by the pup. Puppies of course should not go to a park or walk down the road until they have had this vital jab at 16 weeks. This advice comes straight from our doctor whom Mum still consults.

They were given a wee stop in van Reenen's pass and of course a few snacks along the way.

I did gain some fame as Mum had bought an issue of the American dog magazine *Dog Fancy*. She sent my photo off and there I am on page 37 (April 1987) with the caption:

*"Springers are versatile dogs; Merlyn who lives in South Africa, is active in charity work, while one of his daughters, Kerry, is showing promise as a gun dog."*

Like most media they got it wrong, I was pictured with one of these *earlier* little ankle-biters as my own kids hadn't yet appeared. More about my charity work shortly.

### Lesson for Humans
1. Versatility is my second name – see quote above.

**Photo reprinted in**
**'Dog Fancy' magazine, USA, April 1987 edition.**
Sadly this publication ceased to exist in 2015 so Mum cannot get permission to reprint the news article.

# MY CHARITY WORK

As Mum Jo worked as marketing officer at The Wildlife Society it was decided sometime in 1985 to open a shop. I was to get involved!! I went to see this shop in the now former Thrupps Centre where lots of people worked constructing a thatched roof in one corner, hung pictures and generally stocked up the place with clothes and gifts. I can't say I was impressed as nothing seemed edible.

One Sunday evening I was taken with Dad dressed in very strange deerstalker hat and lots of perfumed ladies in bright silk dresses. They called this a Rehearsal. My friend Aunt Charlotte was in charge of what they called a fashion show. I had met her at home several times and particularly liked her young son Robbie who liked walking on our boundary wall, as I did.

Ah, there was a lady I could relate to: who looked like my Mum on an early Sunday morning in a dressing gown, clutching a candle in a saucer and some loo paper trailing out of her pocket. She represented "looking for the loo" at night in one of the small game reserves, before everything got fancy and bathrooms were "en-suite". There would be a separate ablution block humans had to go to, if you had to "go".

Excuse the pun.

It was a mixture of the serious with the funny side of people in the bush. So they had to have me, didn't they, to help "the explorer" or "white hunter" Dad was trying to be. I didn't need any fashion gear. I could just be myself.

The next evening was a great success and I was up and ready to go the minute Dad told me we were off. Mum had been organising eats and getting the place tidy.

After a lot of talk with the big boss Vincent giving a speech and the Vice President's wife, Irene, cutting the ribbon; the show was on. We had to walk between the guests along a corridor outside other shops, which were closed by this time.

I did quite a good performance of sniffing out anything I could find with my nose to the ground like one of those Blood Hounds and Dad with a torch peering all over the place. I rather liked the especial applause I received. Next day there were a lot of photos in *The Star,* our local paper. As I was still small Dad had to lift me up in his arms for a group photo, not giving me the profile I would have wished.*

As they couldn't accommodate all the guests in this small place the first time, the action was repeated the following evening. This time Dad had a meeting and Mum had to put on her safari gear and some brightly coloured socks and with her binoculars round her neck, pretended to be a bird watcher. At night? Were there going to be owls or something? Oh well, I was always ready to help and acted out my part again. On both occasions I was fed something from the buffet, or a tasty morsel would conveniently fall from a paper plate.

_____
* My embarrassment at being cuddled (as you already know, I wasn't the cuddly kind) meant I got an unforeseen erection which shows up in the photo!

## Lesson for Humans

1. Perhaps Springers ought to be allowed to be stars of stage and screen?

With gun and dog into the jungle of Johannesburg. This "explorer" was part of the fun fashion parade organised to celebrate the opening of the Wildlife Society's new shop.

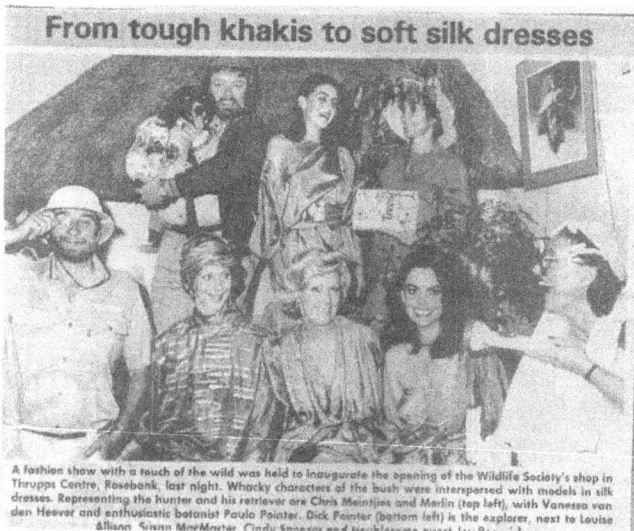

From tough khakis to soft silk dresses

A fashion show with a touch of the wild was held to inaugurate the opening of the Wildlife Society's shop in Thrupps Centre, Rosebank, last night. Whacky characters of the bush were interspersed with models in silk dresses. Representing the hunter and his retriever are Chris Meintjies and Merlin (top left), with Vanessa van den Heever and enthusiastic botanist Paula Pointer. Dick Pointer (bottom left) is the explorer, next to Louise Allison, Susan MacMaster, Cindy Spencer and Necklaware

**Photos by *The Star*.**

20

# HELPING OUT AT WILDLIFE TRAVEL

The next month, April 1st, sadly Vincent resigned from the Society. At first Mum thought it was just an April fool's joke, but sadly she was wrong. She came home more cross than I had ever seen her most evenings. She was soon trying to branch out to start a travel business.

While still at the Society she booked a table at the Sandton Sun hotel that organised the first safari show *ever* over two days on a weekend. The idea was if you sold a trip to someone; some of the profits would top-up the very low bank balance at the Society.

Dad took me along there to say hello to Mum and another nice lady who loved dogs, Anne Marie.

How he got me into not only the car park at the Sandton City (a shopping mall) but walking along past the entrance to the hotel and shops is a mystery these days but along to the big hall where they hold meetings we went. I think I resisted the temptation to lift my leg but my memory isn't perfect.

Oops I was not allowed in! Dad who was good with "the chat up line", asked a lady at the entrance to hold my lead for a few minutes while he went in to find Mum's stand and tell her he couldn't stay as I was forbidden to enter.

Well that wasn't going to deter me. How dare they not allow *moi* inside this big room? It looked like somewhere I should investigate.

I soon yanked on my lead. I was free. Trailing my lead (which might have tripped someone up) I then sniffed my way round all these tables and within seconds landed up jumping up enthusiastically in front of the table to say hello to Anne Marie and my Mum and Dad. Well I certainly was an attraction and people who hadn't already come to get a leaflet soon did so. Naturally this wasn't allowed and Dad soon beat a hasty retreat, this time with me behaving like the model Springer I was . . . sometimes.

Anyway it was time for my tea (as in meat and biscuits if that was all I was getting) so I was anxious to get home. There hadn't seemed much to eat around there.

*Lesson for Humans*

1. Obviously my human hadn't learned – *Don't leave me alone.*

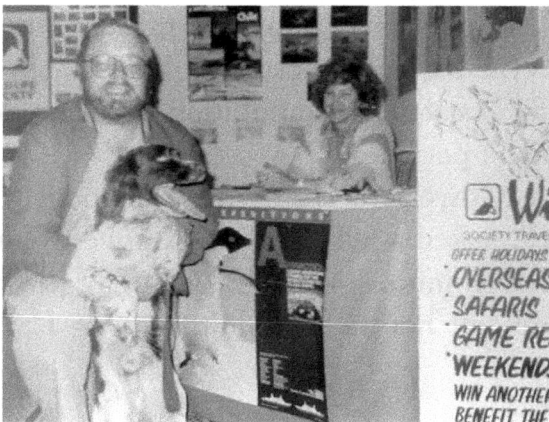

*I found my way in to the travel show at Sandton City. No-one was going to stop me. Seen here with my Dad and Aunt Anne-Marie.*

# THE CROCODILE RIVER

One Sunday off Robyn and I went with Mum and Dad to see friends who lived near this big river out in the countryside a long way from where we lived.

The Humans were to float down the river on inner tubes which are inside big car tyres.

In those days there was no pollution and I, who am a water-loving dog, but, of course not keen on an actual soap-and-water-bath, soon leapt in the river. Eventually the humans got organised and both us dogs were set to swim downstream alongside our Humans, or if we got tired could each perch on an inner tube with one of them.

Well, it was quite a long way and I got tired so clambered onto Dad's tube and perched between his legs so he couldn't see where he was going. I was the captain of this craft so I could steer. There were a few obstacles to be negotiated but I was sure I could do that too.

Mum kept yelling "Where's Robyn?" The current was quite gentle then so Dad said he was sure she would look after herself and be okay. I couldn't sit all the time so managed to have my back legs on Dad's tum and stand in front on the tube and wag my stompy tail enthusiastically in his face as we sailed along.

In those days all dogs like me had tails docked almost the day we were born.

Even Mom was getting shivery by the time we reached a certain part of the river and a vehicle waited to give us a lift back.

Fortunately Robyn was all right and had swum to an island in the river from where she kicked up a fuss. Years later Mum was approached by a kayaker who said he'd heard a large Springer crying loudly. He gave her a lift back to where the others had stayed behind on the river bank.

We both deserved being rubbed down with our towels to get dry and have a good *braai* before we got Dad to drive us home. Mum was very relieved to see her beloved Robyn while I felt very smug about my achievements sailing on this unstable craft.

*Our River Rafting day with Dad on an inner tube which was excellent for me to sit on and wag my stompy tail in his face as I captained the craft down the Crocodile River. My wife Robyn in foreground.*

# MY FIRST EASTER OUTING

A colleague at Mum's work had booked the Easter weekend at Magoebaskloof Hotel but couldn't take up the booking so pleaded with Mum to take it up or she would receive no refund. They allowed dogs. "Woof" I said, meaning "Let's go".

Mum had never been up this way but Dad knew it would be lovely for walks with lots of hills, lakes and waterfalls.

We ended up hurrying off on Good Friday. As ever I was ready to go as soon as I got out of my basket.

Mum packed a box for me with my favourite food, favourite toy, a squeaky tiger at the time, my lead and a ball or two. Oops they realised half way there, my box had been left behind. The only shop open was a small corner shop in a nearby village which sold "everything". They got a very pretty bowl for me with zebras running round the rim and even bought mugs to match which I think are still in their picnic basket. Also some dog tins, and they even remembered to buy a tin opener as it was long before the days of a ring-pull lid. But only a rather flimsy lead was available.

I was allowed into the dining room and kept under the table. I only wangled this because I was a still of an age where I might forget my toilet duties if left in the bedroom or might conjure up some other mischief, if left on my own.

Fortunately a few snacks would come my way. Except for surprising a waiter by suddenly erupting from under the large overhanging tablecloth with a bark – which Dad said was not acceptable – life was rather boring for an active six-month-old like me. I was tethered by this lead. Well as you know when in a tight spot and lots of time on your paws, make your escape – a bit of chewing through the leash did the trick. Dad had to sacrifice his leather strap from the heavy camera bag he used to sling over his shoulder. Now he clasped his bag like a handbag with short loops on either side.

We had a lovely weekend and I was exceptionally good if I say so myself. I never pooed in the wrong place. Mum would put on her dressing-gown at daybreak, put me on the "lead" and we would walk down two flights of stairs to the grassy patch near the front entrance. One morning it was raining but "needs must".

The Tzaneen area was full of lovely smells and sights. We saw endless waterfalls while exploring the area.

It wasn't long before this hotel caught fire and was closed for rebuilding in a very modern way which Mum has since visited. Once more we were in the right place at the right time as I'm sure dogs are no longer permitted.

Of course when we got home there was my box on the kitchen table.

≈≈≈

A quick P.S. to my chewing ability. I don't like waiting.

We were all in Dad's old Mercedes going somewhere on a Sunday morning. He parked the car in Greenside to fetch something. Mum and I were left sitting for a few minutes. Mum was reading the newspaper and I was supposed to be amusing myself in the back seat. Yes I was!

When Dad returned he tried to put on his seat belt. It came away in his hand. I had found a chewy strap attached to the side of the car and munched straight through it.

Mum was in the dog box as much as I was.

*Aren't I so cute at Magoebaskloof on my first Easter even if my parents did forget my food box!*

# MY "AVERAGE" DAY

I was left at home "alone" as the saying goes. I do not like be alone or later, as my family expanded, alone without Humans around. They are always good for chivvying up to take me somewhere, give me a treat, a cuddle – if I must succumb to such frivolities – or be there when I wake from a nap. **But don't leave me on my own.**

This was not good news for my neighbour, an elderly lady professor, I knew as Aunt Hertha. She would even climb a ladder to chat to me over the wall as she had owned two Springers earlier in her life, one was called Splash.

Mum asked for this dog's photo as a keepsake after she died many years later aged 93.

She alerted my parents to this awful noise I made yelping and crying when left alone. Mum, at least, would return from work to give me my lunch during her own lunch-hour. She asked permission to take me to this conservation society when she wasn't out running errands. I would sit in her first floor office overlooking the lovely Delta park with its acres and acres of grass, bushes and trees. I would occasionally sneak down to the heavy front door and escape, despite everyone being given instructions not to let me out.

There was always some unsuspecting delivery man who would oblige. Mum would act like a rabbit, running after me, much to the laughing stock of any staff as I was always far ahead of Mum's attempts to catch me.

Her boss Vincent could see me out of his window and I think the two of us did much to amuse him too. Once I was caught out with this interesting smell. I had to lift my leg and wee. That saved me from a hiding by Mum as she was so thrilled that here I was, getting all grown-up and had lifted my leg. That slight delay meant she caught up with me and put my lead on. She had to phone Dad immediately to tell him the news how grown-up I was when she was back in the office rather than scold me.

Yes in those days "training" was all about "you dog, you do as I want or else". No praise for when I was quite often good. I did love Delta Park and my parents took me to a road near the main entrance Mum used every day to go to work which overlooked the three man-made dams at the bottom of a slope. I would hurtle out of the car, through the gate and launch myself into the last and largest dam. I did love my swimming.

I found the Egyptian Geese, "gypos" for short would annoyingly take off and land a few yards away from me. That was all fine with me, I would just swim after them and the process was repeated with me going in circles but too far out in the water for a human to get me to dry land. I could do this for some 45 minutes which seemed to cause some annoyance as the yelling got louder and louder from the bank.

Eventually this problem was relayed to Lionel who had to scratch his head for a solution despite his ability to train guide dogs for the blind – a job he'd had when he first arrived from the UK to work for Gladys Evans who started this worthwhile institution.

He also said he had brought the first Springers into South Africa, I think he meant the working variety – like *moi* – of English Springer Spaniels.

There are the heavier set, more pompous looking guys with long ears looking rather like the Stuart Kings of England in those stodgy portraits wearing wigs who are called Show Springers.

So Lionel was on my walk. I am none the wiser what is to follow. This time I am on a lead until the water's edge and then released. I dived in as usual and swam on and on with the pesky birds taking off and landing. Dad started calling but I kept on swimming. Mum called. No I was busy I said to myself. After the third request I suddenly sank.

"What the – *dog swear word* – is happening?" I spluttered coming up gasping.

Lionel had started reeling me in with the fishing line he had secretly attached to my collar. Oh, that was nasty as I glugged in a lot of pond water. They tried this trick again without the line, then with the line. I now knew what would happen so I had to say "Ciao" to my bird pals and come ashore quite promptly.

My Mum and Dad both came on walks together as Mum said she couldn't cope on a walk with just me and her alone. Sometimes Dad would be busy or just catching up on sleep after working late so Mum had to bring me by herself. Once near this dam was a lovely patch of undergrowth and I found something interesting which meant I was required to hunt in there.

Occasionally the tip of my stompy tail would show that I was having the time of my life as the white piece showed me wagging it in hunting mode, nose to the ground of course. Apparently the vets who used to dock tails made sure there was a white section (or flag) so we could be seen by our owner.

Finally after 20 minutes or so of whistling, shouting etc., Mum was in tears and drove home to Parkhurst to fetch Dad who was having a siesta. There were neither cell phones in those days nor convenient houses for her to ask the owner to phone him. So the round trip to fetch him must have easily taken another 40 minutes. He was furious from the moment he heard about this but I was still busy. Eventually his deep baritone voice demanding I make an appearance "this very minute" penetrated my now tired little self.

I knew the game was up and meekly came out of the scrub to "face the music".

On another famous outing to the Parkhurst recreation centre, which takes up about two square blocks, I was now with Mum and my "wife" Robyn while Dad was away hunting with my daughter, Kerry, as a better behaved "good gundog". While Mum was chatting to someone in the park, as it was very social for humans and dogs to hobnob, I vanished.

I had been rather crafty and headed downhill to the dead end of one road which leads to a small river or *spruit.* There I could have a swim and run in much more exciting grass full of new sniffs where people and dogs walked daily. A passer-by said he thought he saw a small dog heading that way so she and Robyn, in tow, on foot, tried to find me but I was too clever for that.

Mum then went back to where she had parked her car and started driving to the other side of the *spruit* which had no access by road. Still there was no sign of me. She called in at the vet, and local shops pointing to Robyn (who looked totally unlike me being mostly white and was a much larger dog).

"Have you seen a dog like this?" What *was* she going to tell Dad who would only be home in *five* days' time?

Eventually she drove home to set the telephone answering machine up in case anyone called before she searched the suburb again. I did wear a name tag on my collar with a phone number, but *no address*. Again this was way before micro-chips were inserted into dogs which we recommend now. She grabbed a drink and gave Robyn a snack. Sometimes the intercom at the front gate didn't work so she went to unlock the gate and for some reason opened it to the road.

"Thanks very much," I muttered under my breath as I was getting bored of sitting there and sauntered in.

I had caught her nicely off-guard as I had found my way home, but had never been by paw the several blocks to the park, or beyond it, without being in the car. No one could have dropped me off.

Mum burst into tears and rewarded me as a prodigal son, with hugs and food. For once I didn't mind a cuddle in my wet and bedraggled state.

# BECOMING A DAD

I kept being reminded with my hormones raging that I was now growing up in body, if not in mind. I could not roam around the neighbourhood as Mum's dog, Bracken, a golden retriever once did. Even at a young age in Germany, Mum remembers her Dad cursing that he had to set out late at night to collect him. Someone had phoned the Colonel that yet again Bracken was lovesick on their doorstep anticipating an amorous adventure with their female dog. He was always grateful to be taken home as he had walked many miles, and then sat outside this house all day without food and water.

Eventually, as mentioned earlier, this glamorous well-bred lady, Robyn arrived. She soon got into an interesting condition again later that year (1985). Lionel was duly furious that Chris and Jo had allowed me to "do my thing". This also caused the poor neighbour, Aunt Hertha, to phone my parents to say I shouldn't be having my way non-stop with Robyn. I was carted off to Mum's work during the day.

My parents started reading up all the literature about the impending family – it was long before the Internet was so useful. "The mother will definitely not want to eat the day she is going to have the pups" said the book. Well no one told Robyn, an experienced Mum that. She thought FOOD was a necessity to fuel her up for the milk-bar she was about to provide.

One Saturday afternoon while Dad took his nap, Robyn got busy digging out a shallow hole behind the outside toilet that all old houses had in those days. Mum heard noises and called Dad. There was my firstborn!

Dad gently led Robyn into the outhouse where a whelping box was prepared and plugged in this pup, who eventually was called Kerry, into her Mum's teat.

Eventually six were born but she seemed to be struggling so my folk rushed all the new family to the vet. They were right. There was another two stillborn pups inside her. After a quick Caesarean operation they collected the family and within an hour or two of the op Robyn, being the perfect mum, nursed her little ones.

Sadly two large pups died in the next 24 hours. We were not sure why. Four remained and I became quite a good father producing toys to distract them from endless feeding on my wife's milk. A couple who ran a restaurant in Rosebank heard about the pups when when my Humans dined there and booked two straight away. When the time came to collect them at eight weeks old, these people had changed their minds. One pup,

*Here I am supervising my pups' feeding time.*

34

soon named Bonnie would go to Chris' former school friend Mike; and as Dad had fallen in love with Kerry she would live with us. They advertised in the paper and told their friends that two pups still needed good homes. While my Humans had to go away for a weekend, an artistic couple came to stay but weren't much good at cleaning up after the pups.

In mid-April they found a home for one boy who was bought by a doctor and his wife in Harrismith.

My Humans would drive him there. That left me to look after pups Kerry and Boy and my wife for a long day. When they arrived in Harrismith, mid-way between Johannesburg and Durban they found these people had bought a tiny cocker spaniel pup who was so small they were alarmed at the size of the Springer pup now aged three months old.

With true Afrikaans hospitality they gave my folk a delicious Sunday lunch after which my parents drove home through a terrifying thunderstorm. The pup's new mum was the grand-daughter of President Steyn of the Orange Free State so my son went to a posh-sounding family!

*You might like to see my Mum with Bracken when she was a 'puppy' herself.*

35

# GRANDCHILDREN

While we are on this rather boring subject of family which got in the way of my usual exploits (and I know the subject can be boring hearing how this or that humans' grandchildren's achievements are doing at school as if they themselves had achieved it); before I knew it my daughter Bonnie had given birth to pups. I think there were nine in the litter.

Mike lived in a cottage on a property almost opposite the old Clay Oven near the busy (and now built-up) Lonehill area. Back then it was comparatively wild round there. We were invited to arrive at tea-time to coincide with possible buyers for the pups as good examples of how us adults looked and behaved.

This was a good excuse for me to take off a-wandering and leave them all to it. Robyn pottered off on an errand of her own as she wasn't averse to a little adventuring too.

I saw from the photos later that one pup was playing with a ball while another carried an empty beer bottle around, showing suitable characteristics I thought.

Naturally there was a bit of scolding when I finally reappeared. Well I was only behaving as Springers will and therefore setting a good example in my book.

Mike ended up keeping two pups I got to know well, Abby (rather touchingly named after my Mum) and

Chaucer. Mike was good at cooking and rather cunning-
ly often invited my Humans around for Sunday lunch.
He would casually suggest they bath his dogs while he
was seeing the potatoes were roasted to perfection. Then
Mum would naturally start brushing them once they
were dry.

If left uncombed we get the most awful tangle behind
our ears which had to be sorted out usually with cutting
the dead woolly fluffy bits away. Mum called it storing
our secrets there. You could tell Mike never really got
round to brushing his dogs, being always out doing good
works at Rotary. He was awarded a Paul Harris medal.
He was also a Major in the Army Reserve; so they went
on raids in Hillbrow, sometimes at night.

Now that's where they should have roped *me* in.

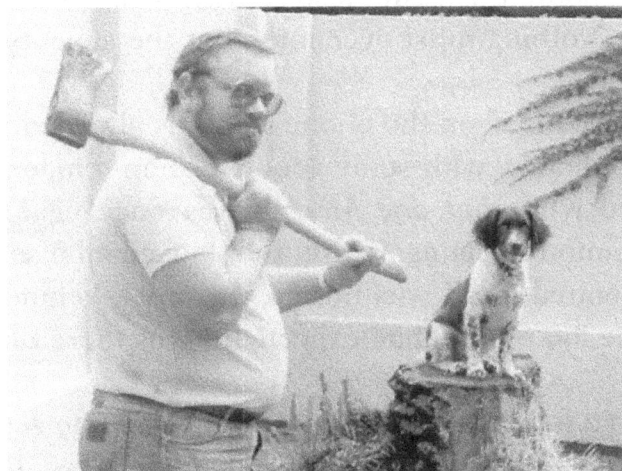

*Here I am helping Dad (Chris)
remove the palm tree stump,
not an easy task at my new
home.*

# THE OUTSIDE LOO

The last episode reminds me that in my youth I was found barking furiously on top of this building. And if truth be told I was a bit scared of being that high. How for the love of bones was I going to get down? Well I had lungs and I soon used them to good effect.

I had found a cat or a bird seeking my attention and after an initial leap I clawed my way up the Virginia creeper to the top.

Now I was in full view of Aunt Hertha's bridge group next door and I am sure I interrupted the bidding on that Saturday afternoon, if I wasn't also giving the old ladies heart failure! Nothing must ever interrupt the sanctity of a Bridge Party!

She duly roused Dad on the phone from his afternoon siesta to immediately, with some good German temper, to go and see why *that dog Merlyn* was once again causing a commotion yet again. My folk looked all over before they spotted me. I was not merely stuck behind the door in the loo as they had expected. I was there *on top!*

Dad brought a ladder and soon carried me down to get my paws on terra firma. I don't remember ever repeating this particular exercise.

# MY DRINKING & EATING QUIRKS

When I first arrived at my new home in Parkhurst, it clearly needed my help to clean up the house and garden as there were two enormous palm tree stumps in the small front courtyard. Friends of my Dad all said these would be easy to remove. They regularly showed up and hacked away at this fibrous material. Usually the axe got stuck by the second swing into this tree trunk by these macho guys. Dick was an Austrian who showed the most determination and he kept returning to do a bit more. He even collected wood wherever he went and as a member of Dad's target shooting/parachuting club "Hågars" (no doubt named after the cartoon *Hagar the Horrible*); he always had a neat woodpile stashed outside his door at home, waiting for the winter weather to light a fire or use on a *braai*.

Dad made sure some encouragement was offered in the form of a *dop* of Jägermeister to assist with further swinging of the axe only for it to stick once more. When the bottle appeared to be empty Dick tipped it up just as I caught a few drips. I was of course helping as always. I really liked the taste!

My first birthday soon came around and Mum had organised an iced cake from one of the corner shops in Parkhurst. There were no restaurants allowed to operate in this suburb then nor were there any cake shops nearby. Now Parkhurst is famous for its cafés.

When she went to collect it, she looked horrified, as the icing was pink with my name on. She told them in suitably annoyed tones "But this is for my boy." They started apologising but she laughed and said "It's for my Springer Spaniel."

I can't remember if this cake was chocolate but I soon developed a liking for chocolate. A friend had brought a cake which was not eaten at a function so Mum popped it in the freezer.

When visitors arrived unexpectedly, Mum dug it out of the deep-freeze and put it on the stove to defrost. On offering the visitors a slice it looked a bit lopsided but she put it down to the melting process as she didn't normally freeze cakes.

When it came time to put it in the fridge the penny dropped, someone had been helping themselves. Sadly the blame fell on me.

After that I was often taken out for my birthday to a café to have chocolate cake or chocolate ice cream as my birthday was 23 November and it was already summer weather in Johannesburg. This was long before they pronounced that chocolate was bad for dogs. I lived to a very ripe old age, longer than Mum has counted with any of the other 12 Springers she's shared her life with.

# BUBBLY

My parents drank a lot of this fizzy stuff, almost more of it than ordinary wine. So when Dad would get ready to push the cork out of the bottle I started yelling in excitement. It would pop out with a satisfying bang and off I would go to retrieve it.

So even if a normal bottle of wine was opened I would start up my excited yap, accompanied by anyone else as my family grew, which amazed anyone coming to eat with us.

'Why this awful noise?' they would enquire.

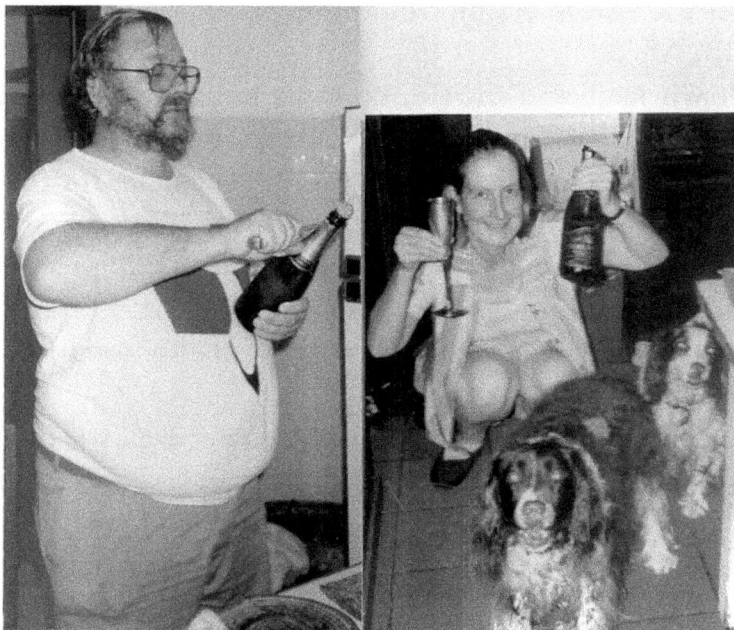

# BY WAY OF . . .

. . . explanation. Maybe I did all these weird things as most people said my parents were rather off-beat, eccentric or just plain weird too. You know what they say about people looking and acting like their dogs! Dad was born under the Gemini sign which meant you laid the blame at the twins' feet. Even Mum sometimes didn't know which twin she was dealing with. He was very creative and always listened to lots of music which led to running some programmes on the new community radio stations including Radio Today and Classic FM – the latter the sister version from the UK – when it started in South Africa.

He worked in advertising concentrating on "below-the-line" which as far as I worked out, meant just about anything from conferences to thinking up clues for treasure hunts, writing scripts and organising music for small films on promoting shopping centres that had yet to be built. This was to attract people who might occupy the shops when the place was finished – "anchor tenants" or something.

As a keen opera singer with regular weekly singing lessons, he would partake in quite a few Gilbert & Sullivan operettas those first years. That meant rushing off to a lot of rehearsals; far more than there were shows. If not rehearsing there were hunting expeditions and he took to leading trips to strange places. He said if a South African passport could make it there (and home safely), like Zaire (now the DRC), he would lead a trip to the Gorillas; or China for Pandas. Mum and I were often left on our own for days or weeks.

Mum also had to turn her hand to whatever funds she could bring in for this conservation society as she was sometimes the sole person in the Marketing department.

It could be setting up a table of goods for sale in a shopping centre on a Saturday morning before the retail shop was opened. And of course, her first love, travel also entered into it.

This led to her new career ultimately running her own travel business. People were very kind and invited them on outings like ox wagon trails – Dad invariably helped cook breakfast over the open fire; trips to the Tuli Block where Mum enjoyed some of her first game viewing and night game drives as well as walks in the bush. Dad saw to it that he serenaded the assembled company with either an aria or a well-known musical number as they sat under the stars in the *boma* (a sheltered area made by twigs or a make shift wall) after dinner round the roaring log fire.

Another was a visit to a guy in the Western Transvaal who farmed and dug up the occasional diamond. He was always popping into the society's office to give his advice – a three-hour drive from home! (Perhaps he flew to Lanseria, a small airport north of Jo'burg?) When he invited Boss Vincent for a weekend, he suggested Mum and Dad went off to keep him company instead of him as he wanted to know if his property would make a suitable commercial place to visit.

During their visit they were flown over Mr X's property and shown the diamond diggings where he could raise some money if he was short of cash, and driven all over the place. His family appeared not to live there often, so while on his own (I can sympathise) he must have suffered from depression. A year or so later he went up a *koppie* (hill), stripped down, shot himself and the vultures had a feast. His family did ultimately start running a game farm.

Another unusual character was Paddy who lived in a castle on the top of a hill in the lowveld and kept baby orphaned rhinos. Dad got on well with him as both collected weapons. Paddy owned an amazing amount of many unusual weapons plus suits of armour in the main "baronial" hall complete with balcony.

He was opening a self-catering house which could have eight people to stay but never could anyone from another race visit. He got hold of Mum to help rent the place out.

It was *all* Mum's fault when a family quite naturally took their African nanny along to look after their small children. Plus she was expected to keep this lodge fully booked when the fridge was only bar-sized.

Sadly, the baby rhinos died anyway of broken hearts or their unusual diet as I don't think anyone at that stage had worked out what was best to feed them on.

Until Robyn arrived on the scene, they then invited house sitters to stay who enjoyed staying at no cost to my Humans, I was parcelled off for weekends, sometimes to Lionel's home, or to a work colleague's wife's sister. I was then handed back with no complaints so if I got into bad habits they stuck. I made sure I was so cute they wouldn't "tell tails".

*Occasionally Chris and Jo had their picture in the paper to promote a destination like Peru. You will notice they had their priorities right: Kerry sits on the chair and the humans plus Holly and me on the floor.*
Photo: *Rosebank Gazette*

# SCHOOL

Dogs, but particularly *moi*, have a good vocabulary of our owners' mother tongue. They say we understand the amount of words a three-year-old child has grasped. It's a pity humans haven't taken a course in dog language. However, I will admit Mum was learning fast especially if we pretended or did vomit in the night or needed the "bathroom" as Americans would say, urgently. "Open the door, Mum and do it even in your sleep."

I didn't like the conversations about "training" or "school". Perhaps because my Humans were so busy as just explained, Lionel said he would take me for several months to live at his house and train me. In hindsight this seemed very odd; even if I learnt something with *him* why would I do it when I got back home?

So off I went and Mum did say that things were very quiet at home at the end of that June. I was now seven months old.

We will skip over this unhappy time. Mum was not there to hear my disapproval of being *made* to do exercises or else . . . (spanking and the like were *de rigeur*) or I am sure she would have rescued me. Lionel was also getting more and more exasperated with me, despite being a trainer of Barbara Woodhouse's calibre, but not her fortune (if she had one).

Mum still has the cartoon that appeared in UK news-papers when Barbara died. There are the dogs sitting on their cloud with halos while Mrs Woodhouse checks up on the rows and rows of well-behaved dogs.

The caption read: *It was heaven, rolling in the dirt, fighting and doing as we pleased. Then Barbara Wood-house came up . . .*

Lionel was going broke and had an unhappy marriage. He was about to move to this small holding south of Jo'burg before ultimately deciding he would return to the UK.

The only story Mum knows is that while loading up the truck with furniture I was told to sit and stay inside the house by the open front door.

Did he *really* think I was going to sit still? Of course *not!* Out the door I dashed and made sure I was difficult to find. I bet he thought what *would* he say to Chris and Jo if I had gone for good?

At that point Lionel said to them, "Merlyn has gradu-ated" and sent me home at the end of July. My parents did sound a bit surprised and impressed as I think school was to last three months. "Oh no, Merlyn was *so good,* I am letting him go early." Years later the truth came out. He sheepishly admitted that I (as well as him) had failed "big time".

There were a few follow-up sessions in our garden with me on a lead (I have the photos to prove it) where I would sit and stay if asked nicely.

I also accompanied Mum to the society so I did one of my Escapes out the door and would not stop. At first she did not worry as I was so "well trained", surely I would come when she whistled?

# Springer Cottage
## Parkhurst

A Home from Home

in the Heart of the Parks

Some people phoned us to see if they could put their dog in the kennels because of the Springer Cottage. We had to say it was an upmarket B&B!

More about this under *Renovations*.

# NOTES ON MY MEMORIES

I am deliberately not writing my autobiography from the day I was born till the day I was sent to "Rainbow Bridge" as it would be similar to how humans do things and as you can see I do everything I can in a completely different way. And I am sure, like a lot of humans, one memory leads to another in your brain.

I should explain Rainbow Bridge is a mythical place like King Arthur's "Avalon"; a place we all pass over to the other side. It is my parent's firm belief that they will be reunited with their dogs who have passed over. When I arrived I met up with Robyn and daughter Kerry and had to round them up to meet Dad when he sadly died in 2013, but more of all that later. He would have been greeted too by Rusty, his parents' red setter, bought as a pup when he was born (1950) and they made a plan to escape their back yard on the mines (Crown Mines where his Dad was mine manager but it was situated out in the *veld* in those days); Chris in his nappy would lift the latch and Rusty would oblige with jumping and pushing a higher bolt off its hook and out they would go.

It was a miracle Chris was born to a mother who was already over 40 who had been one of the first radiographers which meant you were unlikely to have kids in those early days. So Rusty took the part of any sibling who might have come along, for which it was too late. His Dad had first married a smart lady who was secretary to Sir Ernest Oppenheimer and moved in society circles which did not work for a "hands-on" type Morton. His mum Trudy (whom Mum had never met) had married someone in the army who after the war helped get Hamburg back on its feet.

The mayor asked the local Count who gave board and lodging to an artist during the war in his Schloß to thank him with a painting. This hung on our wall all the time I lived in Parkhurst; it was very brooding of the North Sea – I guess it was reminiscent of how the Germans felt after the war with so many homes to rebuild and little to eat.

He was called Major van Rooyen and was already succumbing to cancer and died in 1949. After that Trudy met up with the now divorced Morton at a social gathering.

*Thirsty work for me and Uncle Dick who also assisted to remove the palm tree stump.*

# PLANES AND BIRDS AND THINGS

I was always very observant of things in the air; particularly birds and insisted on a front seat in a car next to the driver, even if that meant standing or sitting on my Mum's lap or even the driver himself, usually Dad.

I remember going to Wonderboom airport north of Pretoria at least once to pick up Aunt Charlotte (as her husband worked for the Natal Parks Board) who often got a last minute seat on the government plane connection from Melmoth (or perhaps Ulundi) which landed there.

Of course she relied on Mum's transport to get her back to Jo'burg. We parked and while walking along the pavement there I could see all these exciting "big birds" take off and land.

I went once inside Jan Smuts Airport (now OR Tambo) to greet a couple who had completed a round-the-world trip which Mum helped organise including a long (semi-circumnavigation) Antarctic cruise. Maybe Dad thought it should also be celebrated with a piper wishing them a warm welcome on the bagpipes. The guys we were greeting were after all Irish.

I know Dad phoned first to find out if this greeting was permissible by the authorities. It caused quite a stir to those waiting to welcome the passengers plus my presence no doubt! I am surprised I didn't howl an accompaniment given the rather strident notes of a bagpipe. I was rather hurt when it was announced not long after that no animals were to be admitted to the airport; only guide dogs would still be allowed.

When I was much older with Robyn and Kerry for company, Dad used to book a friend's cottage on a game farm in the direction of Welgevonden north-west of Jo'burg. He would sometimes treat Mum and us to a two or three-night outing during the week as he was by then working *every* weekend for Classic FM on a four-hour shift. It also required him to be in an hour before that. He was exhausted by the time he got home so you could say weekends were a "write off", as Mum was too nervous to take me out when he wasn't around after my previously mentioned behaviour in the park.

This time Cousin William (on Mum's side of the family) was doing a lightning visit flying back from Buenos Aires to Johannesburg and later that day due to catch a flight to his home in Yangon. We picked him up early that day so he could do some urgent shopping and gave him a big lunch. Then, as we were en route to this game reserve, we all piled in the car to take him to the airport. At the drop-off place outside the departure terminal I thought this was the start of an expedition.

I hopped down onto the pavement. It always seemed to be *me* in trouble. The others dutifully stayed in the back of the *bakkie* (pick-up truck) the "goody four paws".

I loved watching the kites fly in the local Recreation Centre (Verity Park). To their credit my Humans did bring me home a kite from China. Sadly I think after one failed attempt, it sat on the bookshelf for years. Eventually after my demise it was given away. It reminded Mum of me and she couldn't bear to look at it.

They were invited in 1990 to a big number birthday Klaus was celebrating. He had chartered a flight on the wartime plane the Junkers Ju 52 which South African Airways used on weekends for pleasure sightseeing flights lasting an hour from Rand Airport. The pilots were all experienced Captains who seized the chance to fly such an amazing antique plane voluntarily.

I was not asked to the birthday party which saw Dad dress up wearing his Biggles type leather flying hat. They were all given mini bottles of champagne to drink while in the air.

Mum phoned up SAA and asked the reservations people if they would permit a small dog on one of these flights. As she was by now running her own travel business full time and with an IATA license (it sounds smart but I don't know what that is), she thought she might wield some influence. Yes they said without any persuasion "If you pay for a seat, we don't mind having a dog as a passenger."

Sadly it wasn't long before the plane was grounded. It needed new tyres for the landing wheels. Mum followed the progress of the repair. She read recently once the tyres arrived but then there were other nuts and bolts needed to put them on which were unavailable.

Sadly that had to stay on my "bucket list" as I had hoped I might borrow the Biggles hat to wear when I was on the plane.

In November 2001 Anne Marie and Mum enjoyed an extraordinary free trip on a DC4 thanks to Transnet which flew almost at treetop height from OR Tambo outside Johannesburg to Swartkops Airport near Pretoria.

They relaxed in very luxurious business class seats and about 20 minutes later they landed on the runway out-side this museum which was about to be re-launched as the Historic Transport Museum while promoting the "Transnet Foundation's Tourism Products". There were speeches, African choirs singing and a lavish amount of food and drink served.

It was while Mum was inspecting the museum she that she saw the Junkers is now mounted on the wall.

Then they were all driven back on a coach after dark to OR Tambo where even the parking fee was paid for their car which had been there since late morning.

All Mum had done to deserve this invitation was book a train tour (part of the SAA group) along the Garden Route for a friend and herself a few years earlier. Both ladies did think this junket was rather "over the top" as far as extravagance was concerned but had, of course, thoroughly enjoyed themselves!

# MY SLEEPING ARRANGEMENTS

As you know I soon put paid to the idea that *I* should sleep in the kitchen all by myself. I managed to sleep more or less where I felt like both for naps and during the night. Of course various baskets were introduced to encourage me to occupy at snooze time.

As I was quite small I often leapt onto Dad's lap for a photo or just to pretend I was interested in posing but really I got a better advantage to see what was happening through a window. While I am in a chair I really like to sit on a person's lap and then lean against them. Springers are great "leaners" and in the kitchen I advise leaning against the cupboard a Human wants to open or trip them up in the hopes some morsel will fall your way.

When I jump on a bed all I can see is one of my parents snoozing under the covers. I have no idea when I lean on a lump in the bed that it's someone's feet or knees which make for a convenient pillow. It's their bad luck if their limb goes numb because I am leaning on it.

I might also stand on the person to give them a wake-up lick on the face and my paw causes a bit of agony standing on an ankle under the blanket. I do know what a Human yelp is like, one of the few expressions that mirror our own word when getting hurt.

One morning Mum had been up early making herself and Dad a cup of tea. She re-entered the bedroom with the steaming mugs and said to a sleepy Chris: "Where's Merlyn got to?"

It was some moments before I emerged from the very bottom of Dad's bed *between the sheets* with heavy covers on top.

They were stunned how there was enough air down there for me to breathe all night? Dad, when he slept well, never stirred so it was very comfy for me.

They read in the books later that Springers are good at burrowing under bracken and other undergrowth so perhaps that's why I felt going down between the sheets was a good idea. My folk had decided on sleeping in two large single beds as Dad had once had a dream about kicking the winning goal in a Rugby match. He had once played in the 1st team for St John's private school. Unfortunately for Mum he kicked her and she woke up yelping and an enormous bruise on her thigh was the result of "the match".

I was just being my *usual* self. Sorry, but I don't read the manuals of what Springers are *supposed* to do.

Another example was my foster son Brecon to whom I hope I was a good Dad. I encouraged him to find a comfy spot or two. Once when he was missing, he was found in the bottom shelf of the cupboard where Mum kept her best jerseys: some bought in South America knitted with alpaca wool or Iceland with lamb's wool, so they were extra soft and allowed just enough space to wiggle in for a snooze. I should add that temperatures in Jo'burg in winter can reach zero or even sub zero. As

Aunt Hertha told my parents a dog's temperature has to be kept at a higher degree than humans. As a professor, her word stood for a lot!

Of course the books say we like our privacy and a secret hidey-hole like digging out a scrape under a bush especially if it's muddy gets first prize. There may be something in that in my next life. By the way Dad always said I lived to a good old age as things were so good on this side, why bother to leave?

*Lessons for Humans*

1. Dogs, especially Springers, like to make themselves comfortable.

*Brecon took to reading Mum and Dad's book on travel "The Borneo Headhunters' Cuckoo Clock".*

# ANOTHER OF MY GOOD WORKS

I think I was "helping" with good works in the year after the shop was launched, Aunt Charlotte had a hand in an interior decorating project which entailed launching a new townhouse complex in Morningside. There were going to be goods for sale, lectures, a *braai* and a fashion show. Perhaps I could be the hunter dog once again?

This was one of the first of the early cluster developments which now occur all over the north of Johannesburg and are now not unusual.

My folk were to walk 10 kms along the Braamfontein Spruit, affectionately known as The Braamies. The starting point was at Rattray Park at the bottom end of Conrad Drive in Blairgowrie with a small round dam. A well-known conservationist, Clive, was to lead the walk from there, along the river to Morningside. This distance which, even then, was quite a hike for my folk. Robyn, my soul mate, had now joined the family so she and I were accompanying them.

I don't like waiting as I think I have mentioned, so bored with all this time on my lead; something grabbed my attention. Ducks! Hurrah!

I jumped into the dam with a big splash, trailing my lead behind me, apparently nearly yanking my Mum off her feet. But I was on a mission.

Eventually all were ready to roll, except me. I was busy swimming to get that duck. The start of the walk was delayed.

After much encouragement by Dad for me to please hurry up Mum had to resort to wading in, grab my lead and haul me out. Apparently this was *her* fault as she had me on the lead originally.

I conveniently shook the water off all over her. Now she had to walk in wet *takkies* (walking shoes) all that way, while us dogs had a lovely walk with photos of us jumping from boulder to boulder to occasionally cross the river.

This walk took much longer than expected and we didn't see much of the festivities that awaited us at the finish. Dad had to rush off to a meeting. We'd all got up very early to park his car there (Mum following in her car) and then return to Blairgowrie where Mum had left her car.

Mum was very cross with Dad after all this effort to be going home immediately. He in turn blamed "little old me".

Later she read out some publicity to me which promoted the regular walks along the *spruit*: "All dogs must be on leads". Surely that had nothing to do with *moi*?

*On our fund raising walk up the Braamfontein Spruit after our delayed start – hardly my fault – it was the duck's!*

# CIRCUITING THE KYALAMI RACE TRACK

We all piled into the car to go and assist the Guide Dogs raise funds one Sunday morning in July 1995. The venue took over 4000 dogs to set a record for the number of dogs in one place. We were all on leads and set off when instructed to circuit the famous Grand Prix race track.

I saw a Panda and a Rhino but they didn't smell like animals so I think they were humans wearing silly out-fits. There was also a St Bernard pulling a cart piled high with at least three or more children.

I like St Bernards ever since I met one on a walk in Delta.

I was such a small guy I walked straight under him. The big dog kind of lost me for a moment and looked a bit surprised as I emerged on his right side instead of his left. They are very gentle guys but I was never scared of approaching any dog. There were certainly enough of us around this racetrack to make new friends.

They did provide water bowls at various intervals although I could have done with a biscuit or two. Kerry got sick the next day and Mum blamed this communal water we all drank.

Maybe she caught something? But I wonder if it wasn't nerves that caused it as she was such a quiet lady and we know what happened when she was stressed during our house renovations.

Fortunately Mum and Dad decided that after one lap, or a circuit of 4.2 kms, that enough had been done for the Guide Dogs. It was time for us all to go home to sleep off our exertions.

*My run down to jump on the garden wall has been wiped out. I am inspecting the foundations for a guest cottage.*

# RENOVATIONS

At least twice in my life my parents turned our home "upside down". This is apparently called House Improvements. Well, they are not to be recommended. I will admit my house was quite small to start and they appeared to want more wash rooms; a separate dining room and a new large bedroom. This went on for about 4½ months with us all sleeping on the floor on a double mattress in the sitting room. This was the only room with a roof over its head – it was winter so no rain was expected but it was cold. As for ablution facilities at the time, there was one tap in the garden in the front and a lavatory which had no walls as it was about to be removed from its former position. Mum could not use it when workmen were around and either timed her visit to the shops where there was a toilet or had a potty behind the bar. This had a high counter in front but caused the builder, Mr Ferreira some puzzlement when he yelled:

"Mrs Chrees (after Dad's name), come and look."
Eventually Mum would emerge trying to look – as if she normally crouched behind things – very nonchalantly. It would usually be to show Mum that something he'd completed was built plumb straight unlike the old house walls. This was apparently a major achievement and

something for which Mr Ferreira had to receive immediate praise.

Just in case you are holding your noses with the smell that you think we all caused, my parents went to the club called affectionately Old Eds and had a shower at lunchtime every day. Dad got quite chatty with other men as he didn't look as if he had run a mile or two first, so why did he need a shower?

Mum had a family friend, Lucy, who invited Mum weekly to have a bath in her lovely home in Hyde Park. How Mum looked forward to those Friday afternoons! She hated showers.

Of course I assisted walking up and down the trenches (where the foundations for the new walls of the cottage would be built) as *my* garden was being encroached upon and *my* favourite shrubbery had been demolished. This had also ruined by launch pad onto the wall.

I did not know what this grey liquid was which appeared to harden after a while so continued pottering along these holes which were deep enough for my endless admiration as to how these huge holes had been dug.

My folk didn't know what I had been up to but they soon found out. Late that evening I let out some ear splitting yelps.

The wretched stuff had hardened between the pads under my paws.

I was hauled off to the late night Vet to have it dug out from between my paw pads along with an injection first to deaden the pain.

I still remained attached to this stuff and my last action – a dog knows when his time has come and I was very ill – before the Big Injection; was to step in the smallest piece of concrete which was around the bottom of some new gum-poles being erected to extend the carport. The poles would hold up new netting, supposedly hail proof to protect the three vehicles they owned.

It caused them much grief to see my paw print in concrete when they returned home that afternoon without me.

Another downside to these renovations was Kerry, my daughter, got ill. She generally slept in the temporary kitchen round the corner from this makeshift bedroom where my parents slept. She yelped in the early hours and Mum shot out of bed to see what was wrong. She was shaking from head to tail. All Mum could do was gather her in her arms and hold her gently.

She kept shaking for ages. So Mum propped herself up on cushions and tried to comfort her all night. At daylight they took her to the Vet and he said it must have been an epileptic fit.

Apparently epilepsy is at least as common in dogs as in humans. He wrote a prescription for calming tablets to be given every day. This would make her really dozy all the time.

These pills were put in her food for a year or two until a Vet, wanting to hear more about Antarctica, a part of the world in which Mum specialised, came to one of their film shows and the buffet supper that went with it. He said it was unnecessary to dope her every day.

So after that they stopped giving her pills. Fortunately this ghastly episode was never repeated. Kerry was such a placid pup that having the house almost pulled down around your ears was not a nice experience for her, or any of us.

*Holly would dig up her water bowl when she was cross! That often left us without water to drink. My parents made a plan with a bowl that she couldn't 'dig up'.*

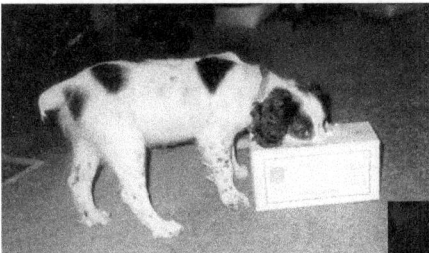

# BATHS

Mum recalls often bathing me. I can't think why I was required to have baths? A bit of mud between family after all my swims is surely acceptable? I don't remember rolling in anything "delightful" which my successors often did, given "half a chance".

The procedure required both parents to administer shampoo and hold me until the elaborate rinsing was finished, which seemed to take forever. There were no water restrictions in those days.

One time I got bored and shook myself vigorously. Mum leapt back and she also yelped. She had put her back out. It was the only time she has ever asked a doctor to call at the house who gave her an injection and she stayed in bed for two days.

Of course I really did her a favour as she went to a lot of physio(therapy) sessions and a therapist emigrating shortly to Tanzania as her husband would be working at the SA Breweries up there, gave her some exercises to do at home. Even in the smallest cabin on a ship pitching and rolling in the Antarctic seas she "religiously" does these few exercises and has not, touch wood, consulted a physio since, for back problems.

*Lessons for Humans*

1. You see how helpful I was!

# HOLLY

Before I knew it we were a family of four. Uncle Mike had seen a Classified Ad in the paper saying there was a Springer up for adoption from the Alberton SPCA. Mum was feeling a bit low that Christmas as her Dad had died in the UK despite the fact they didn't really get on, but they did write to each other. Perhaps more hurtful was she was disinherited whatever that meant. So she said to Chris "Well one more dog won't hurt!"

After much enquiring as to where this pup was as over Christmas these people don't seem to answer the phones; it turned out one of the kennel maids had taken her home for Christmas. She had been found half starved in the *veld* and handed in by a passer-by.

We named her Holly after one of my ancestors as well as the Christmas theme.

I soon knew she was one after my own heart. At a *braai* they had before New Year, she was drinking coffee out of a mug that was put on the ground, photographed cuddled up to an empty bottle of wine and generally making herself at home.

One drawback was she loved water. When she was cross she would "dig up" her water bowl or that's what Mum called it. So with this furious splashing in this large bowl it would empty all the contents. And we'd be left with nothing to drink. That's not too clever on a hot day but I couldn't stop her. A large washing up size bowl was bought and the bottom cut out, and then turned upside down.

"*Now* what *are* they doing?" I thought.

The water bowl was then positioned inside this cut out hole which helped to balance it and keep some water inside for us to drink.

She also found the place Mum stored boxes and paper to eventually recycle. She particularly liked tissue boxes as she was sure some food must be inside. She would even go around with it on her head bumping into furniture – I tried not to laugh.

Mum regularly made Dad tea or coffee and put it on his desk while he was usually on the phone. She would then carry on with her travel work around the corner in the library area.

"I thought you made me coffee," Dad boomed one morning.

"Yes I did," she replied equally loudly.

"Well where is it?" The mug had been full. Now it was completely empty. Not a drop had been spilled. She pointed to this small dog curled up on his visitor's chair in front of his desk and told Dad to keep quiet.

"You must let sleeping dogs lie."

Another day she made Holly her own coffee (not too hot) and allowed her to lap from a mug with a Springer picture on the outside. We have the photo to prove it. Not a drop was spilled.

Holly was also something of a magician; she often attended board meetings in the lounge which doubled as a meeting place when Dad had clients. This time our friend Bridget arrived who marketed dog products, mainly a famous biscuit brand and conditioning tablets. I think they were sort of vitamin pills. She was always very generous in leaving us some samples just in case we didn't like a biscuit with a new flavour, we could of course complain. Along with this was a large cardboard box of the bottles (each in its own small box) containing the pills.

Dad had not put the pills away and came back to find a sleeping Holly next to an empty bottle. How had she extricated it from the big box, got one small box out, then undone the screw cap before she ate the contents?

I was really proud of this little girl and glad she had been rescued by the SPCA and we in turn had given her a home. Sadly no thoughts of hanky panky for me; at six months she had to be spayed. Part of the fee my folk had paid, and documents they had signed, agreed to having her spayed. So back she had to go for the operation.

*Lesson for Humans*

1. So it wasn't just me who was a bit eccentric.

*Holly joins the family as an abandoned pup through the SPCA and soon makes herself at home drinking coffee.*

# ...PLAYS CROQUET

Soon after their divorce, Mum joined several organisations so she could have a social life. The University of the 3rd Age (U3A) started at the end of 2000. Jonathan Paton (son of Alan Paton) said he could lecture in literature and also teach croquet. Mum had hated this game as a child but she thought "why not?"

Brecon and Holly went wherever she could take them during the week she had "custardy" which included playing croquet once a week at Bruma bowls club in Johannesburg. They sat quietly on the boundary line until Mum had played a few games and they joined in when there was a break for tea and biscuits. Holly was now keen to go home but another game was being played. She came across to Mum and, despite never being keen on balls, picked up Mum's heavy blue ball (it weighs about 1 lb; six times heavier than a 2½ oz tennis ball – we won't go into the metric as we can't work it out exactly and we don't want a "proof" of mathematicians' complaints). Not only that, the diameter of a tennis ball is eight inches (20 cms) compared to the 11½ inches (29 cms) width of a croquet ball.

She picked it up and carried it over to place at the mouth of the hoop. She had worked out they must run hoops in order to get on with the game. The rest of the players stood back in amazement while Mum was totally embarrassed. She gently said: "No Holly, I am not allowed to do that," and replaced her ball.

"No," Holly insisted; promptly picked up the same ball and *again* put it by the hoop.

Holly, was found as a stray sadly didn't have an exact wuffday so Mum made it the 10th October as it would be nearly the right date she would have been born. It was also then a public holiday; the birthday of Paul Kruger. She kindly bought a chocolate cake to share with the players at their tea-break.

*Kerry comforting Cousin Bennie after her stroke.*

# THE CIRCUS

One day I was in the car when my folk drove past a lovely green park near Cresta shopping centre. I think they have probably made it into a car park now as they have with Rattray Dam, just in case you want to swim after ducks.

There parked on this lawn were some caravans, trailers and people seemed to be unfolding a huge tent. A person led a large grey animal out of a trailer with a long trunk. I can't get Mum to help translate my doggy language suitably into human words; I was lost for woofs with my eyes popping out. What a huge creature!

By now Dad had stopped the car so I could take in all the sights.

I have a feeling the animal raised his trunk in salute as if to say: "If only we were all free creatures in this world."

I felt I had met a kindred spirit and was not at all scared of the elephant.

*Lesson for Humans*
1. In an ideal world all animals would be free.

# NOW IN MY 17th YEAR . . .

My folks threw a party for my 10th birthday as they thought that I had lived (batted) a pretty good innings, that meant I was 70 in human years. Before they knew it in 1997 they had to throw a 14th year party for *me!* Mum got her priorities right as everyone arrived with biltong and other treats for us dogs who got served before she and Dad offered refreshments to the guests.

For some reason everyone thought this party for dogs was very amusing and the parties raged on into the night when all I wanted was a quiet corner to sleep.

Now in 1999 we were all to see Gavin again who made an annual "pilgrimage" to see his parents and visit the bush which he missed since he now lived in Switzerland. These visits to friends in Jo'burg were very rushed so everyone usually met at a pizza restaurant.

This time in January my folks were going to a fish restaurant in Rivonia. Dad phoned them and said there was a very special small dog who would be no trouble, and may he be a guest too? This was in the era when dogs definitely had to stay home.

So off we went and Gavin and I remembered each other from *braais* at our house, and the famous camping trip, told elsewhere. Now I could also greet his eldest son, James, who was about seven, on his first trip to South Africa. I really was very good, well I had to be on a lead, but picked up a few scraps or was fed some fish and chips under the table.

So I felt I broke down another barrier as there are now quite a few dog-friendly cafés all over Parkhurst and neighbouring suburbs. Water is provided in a communal bowl and sometimes doggy snacks can be purchased.

≈≈≈

In the middle of 1999 Mum and Dad were invited to a private house in the lowveld, near Pilgrims Rest which some of these big corporate companies own. I think Mum said I must get invited too as I was advancing in years and how many expeditions were left in which I could participate?

The rest of the family remained at home which now included a new pup, Brecon (more about him later), with a house-sitter of course, but *I was invited!* The host was Mark and lots of other people were there. We knew Mark and Yolanda very well as they lived down the road from us in Parkhurst and Dad had sung at their wedding not long before. Mark was always arranging exciting events, like playing croquet on his birthday.

We only left home at dusk on the Friday so the real exploring started on Saturday. I accompanied Mum and a Jack Russell, called Bell, for walks all over the place, near a dam negotiating a few bridges and up a steep slope to enter a disused mine cave. Mum pronounced that "I was as good as gold." I was just tired; my age was starting to show so I curled up on Mum's bed after a good dinner. Sadly I missed the main event.

Mark, Dad and the other guys went out shooting a wild pig that night which were pests, or at least very prevalent on this vast property. I was woken up by the noise when they returned very late that night and was cross I'd missed out on the hunting expedition.

Nevertheless next morning I inspected the kill, now hanging upside down from a tree and was happy to take the credit in a photograph or two.

*A day out  to mourn at Uncle Vincent and Aunt Jane's place in the Magaliesberg after dear Robyn had died. From left: Kerry, Holly and me with my Mum Jo.*

# ROBYN AND KERRY

Sadly I was to lose the companionship of these two great ladies before my own end which was not long after my daughter Kerry. Robyn had been given to us by Lionel when he left for England to live her life out in comfort. As you have read I had other ideas and she raised her last family with us before Mum made sure she was spayed. No more fun for me!

One day in the local recreation park Mum thought she looked sick, although Robyn had been to the Vet a few hours earlier, Mum decided at 5 p.m. another check would do no harm. Mark, the head doctor, took one look at her and said he thought it was her spleen.

He would stay late and operate to remove it. This he did which saved her life for the moment but weakened her constitution as the spleen catches all the germs and deals with them. We knew her days were numbered.

Late one evening some months later, she bled profusely all over the carpet in the hallway. My folk were sleeping until I woke them and they saw what had happened. Robyn was so grateful and knew she had caused a nuisance, licking Mum's hand all the way to the Emergency Vet.

My folk explained about her medical condition and the vet said she could do no more. Sadly they took the decision to give her the Big Injection.

The next day Dad left for a work assignment in Hong Kong. Mum was both cross and very sad he could "take off like this". Incidentally the people there never did pay him. They promised to pay shortly after he returned a week later and here was a generous present of a lacquered inlaid fire screen which Mum could hardly bear to look at.

Very kindly good conservation pals, the former Big Boss, Vincent, and his wife Jane said Mum must go to their hideout, Windhover, in the Magaliesberg to relax for the day and get some exercise.

Mum roped in Anne Marie to go with her with a packed lunch and snacks for us: me, Kerry and Holly.

That was another great adventure and what better way to say our farewells to dear Robyn en route to Rainbow Bridge.

Kerry had some eye problems and went blind in one eye which is an affliction well known to Springers. Mark, our chief Vet, suggested removing the bulging blind eye which he said was probably giving her a headache. This was done and she could even catch a ball, if she did not have two balls in her mouth at once, one sticking out like a lopsided cigarette. Even when blind in one eye it was her job to collect up either the breakfast bowls, the large plastic ones, or the small red ones at tea time and stack them inside each other. Sometimes they were just piled into her basket in the corner of the kitchen but at least she had helped with the dishes.

Suddenly she developed a strange illness, Uncle Mark, our vet, called it Auto Immune Disease which he had very seldom come across in 20 years as a doctor. So her precious white blood cells were being eaten up by her body and she had no defence against illness. He was doubtful any medicine would help as she was already quite old.

One Sunday morning Mum left her in her basket after breakfast while she had an extra nap. A bit later she realised Kerry hadn't stirred and was desperately ill. Once again she and Dad hurried off to the Vet with Dad carrying Kerry to the car. They went straight to the operating room. While Dad was explaining they feared the worst and to please hurry to prepare the Big Injection.

Mark felt for a vein to administer the needle.

There was none. She had died on the table. As in her life she had caused no trouble (unlike some of us) and saved my parents this last expense.

As a happier epitaph Mum remembers Kerry, a very undemonstrative dog, suddenly leaping into Cousin Bennie's arms. They had met Bennie through a travel lecture Dad gave monthly and since they were both Meintjes it wasn't hard to work out they were distant cousins.

Coincidentally they both used the same kind of Pentax camera and Bennie gave Dad a camera and lens she wasn't using which saved some of the effort of constantly changing lens when he was on some Arctic expedition saving his fingers (or Mum's as she often changed lens for him) from frostbite.

Luckily they were introduced to some of Bennie's other cousins because it wasn't long before she was struck down with a series of strokes and had to live in the frail care of one or other retirement homes. She could no longer read or talk.

But she loved to be taken out for lunch and sit in the garden enjoying watching the birds flying around. It was during a lunch at our house in the garden when Kerry took it upon herself to leap into her arms.

We have the photo to prove it with Bennie's lopsided smile.

It has now become quite common for dogs to detect illness or an oncoming seizure and to help, as guide dogs do, if someone has other disabilities than being blind.

Back in my time, in the last century, this was most unusual.

*Sad times when blindness afflicted my daughter Kerry; the vet said it was better to remove the bad eye. She still collected the bowls after our afternoon snack and could catch a ball.*

# MY LATER YEARS

From the early 90s when Mum sold the first travel
agency she had started they began began to travel more
and more. I believe it was to places like the Far Side of
Antarctica reached from Australia and another time a
cruise around the sub Antarctic islands of New Zealand.
These were particularly long trips and sometimes a
series of house sitters came to stay.

Of course we didn't go anywhere for the duration of
their trip either by paw or by car.

The gardens in Parkhurst are so small there was very
little to do; I already knew every nook and cranny; I
became extremely frustrated.

Most of my house sitters were lovely ladies: it was the
only time Mum allowed Dad to befriend ladies playing in
the orchestra of a musical in which he was performing.

Particularly useful was the Wits Orchestra (part of the
University of the Witwatersrand) where he appeared in
*Carousel* and as Orpheus in *Orpheus and the Under-
world'*; he had to vanish through a keyhole! That was a
particularly funny part as he was rather large. Mum set
off the whole audience giggling as she and her pals at the
performance they attended saw Dad swinging in his
hammock on stage at the start, before the lights came up,
as the head god relaxing on Mount Olympus.

The hammock didn't swing at all with its heavy contents – Dad! I digress.

He met Julia and Vanessa, both students, who played various instruments. They were both very nice to us. Vanessa had the habit of letting me have a spoon of her plate of ice cream; then she had a spoonful, then my turn. Mum saw this in operation once and was horrified as to the lack of hygiene.

Sadly there was a very strict lady and we had a mutual dislike of each other. She told "tails" and said to Dad that I had growled at her.

After a particularly long time away when during the day we were either shut inside or outside I was very grumpy. Also if I was inside I had "to go" and the house smelled nicely of my wee on their return. After their divorce Mum installed an extra security gate with a Springer size hole in which they could come and go as they pleased. One of us was measured for his/her vital statistics. When Emily and Nina came to stay they had to have another dog demonstrate how it worked.

Two unpleasant things happened. I was hauled off to the Vet and my private parts investigated. He said I had enlarged prostate glands and they would solve the problem by "de-knackering" me; the gland would then reduce in size of its own accord.

This became a subject at dinner party conversations my parents either gave or attended. If the men had not heard that this story alluded to me, a dog, they looked horrified, as, of course, enlarged prostates are quite common in men of a certain age and they thought they might have to lose "their knackers".

The operation was duly done and in fact they now encourage it should be done to all boy dogs sooner than later unless we are going to be used for fathering the next generation. It is unfair with all the testosterone running around inside us to keep us waiting for some "action".

Worse news was they consulted a well-known dog therapist who can't be named as she is still working today. What she told Dad to do was inexcusable and of course would not, like the days of choke chains for leads, be acceptable today. I don't care; it was beyond any dog code of conduct.

I was to be rolled over with my paws in the air and Dad would lean over me holding my front paws and glare down at me. This was supposed to make me submissive. This activity would be done several times a day for several minutes at random moments when I had not been guilty of any misdemeanour.

I think Dad was very lucky I submitted to this awful treatment and did not bite his nose off.

Mum absolutely hated it and pleaded with him not to do it, or to stop if he did. Sadly Dad was very stubborn and would *not* listen to her, much to his detriment when they got divorced not long after, which he claimed he hadn't foreseen at all.

While we are on these sad subjects, I was diagnosed with mouth and nose cancer all at once in 2000, a few months after Kerry died. Again there was nothing the doctors could do for me. I must live out my life as best I could. I survived past Brecon's first birthday on 9th April.

He had a very handsome cake in the shape of a big bone; it was chocolate of course and Mum helped him blow out his one candle.

We invited his breeder with small daughter; Anne Marie with her grandchild, Kelly who was about eight years old and Mike of course. It was one of the last grand occasions with Dad there too.

Mum and Dad agreed not to divorce until after I died. I was finally put to sleep with the Big Injection when my quality of life had decreased to such an extent that it was no longer worth my while staying on this side of the world.

I, too, must soon cross Rainbow Bridge.

My day came on 5 May 2000, aged 16½, for the Big Injection. I was taken for one last walk at the recreation centre with Dad telling Mum and I to hurry up as we'd made an appointment before the Vet officially opened at 3 p.m. Dad had hurried us so much Mum forgot her tissues. I remember we still had to wait while an elderly lady queue-barged with her dog and kept passing the "time of day" much to my folks' annoyance.

At least Mum or Dad or, both of them, always sent us on our way with a final goodbye, however sad it was for them.

Earlier that week Mum had said goodbye for me on email so later that day the condolences poured in for me from all over the world. Mum still has a scrap book full to prove it.

People said, "You have the other dogs (Brecon and Holly), to keep you company and each other." How wrong they were; things behind closed doors were very tense indeed.

*Brecon at his first birthday with Uncle Mike, Aunt Anne-Marie, her grand-daughter Kelly, Dad Chris, Aunt Lucy, Ken and Alison and Aunt Sally. Inset his bone-shaped birthday cake with one candle.*

# RELIGIOUS OUTINGS

Mum and Dad did take us to the Animal Anti-Cruelty rescue shelter once and it was a sobering experience and rather scary running on the open grass beside the kennels to say nothing of being rather tactless in front of these poor caged animals. It was St Francis Day and we were all going to be blessed. The fee my Humans paid would help their funds.

Another St Francis Day came and we went to Rhodes Park in Kensington and I think Aunt Bridget was there as she had told us about it. This was in aid of the SPCA and Mum saw her former boss (who was one of the many after the Big Boss Vincent) who made them use one tea bag for all twenty members of staff. He was now manager of one of the SPCA branches.

Anyway there were prizes to be won and Mum entered me for a contest for which dog can lift their leg the highest in relation to his size.

Sadly for Mum who is very competitive I failed. I do wee a lot and often wee higher than my own height but by that time I'd run around trailing my lead sniffing and weeing like mad as it was all so exciting, I had peed myself out. So I don't think I even managed to lift my leg at all when the time came to be judged.

In recent years Mum took all the dogs – it must have been the six of them, prior to Bramble and Hugo's time

– to a church in Parkhurst and a lady priest blessed them all on the pavement.

Each dog was given a certificate with their name and a prayer on. Mum kind of hoped that Sally who was already blind might have her sight restored in some kind of miracle. She was always so patient with her disability unlike her brother Ben, who fortunately was older and became blind later in age than his younger sister.

*Colour coded Springers – Bramble and Hugo's family.*

# POLITICS

Goodness you wouldn't think I would be involved one minute in Religion and now have a Political view!

I deputised that my daughter Kerry go and vote. I am not joking. At the end of April 1994 was the first democratic election in South Africa which lasted three days amongst some horrors like a bomb blast at our international airport, Jan Smuts (now renamed OR Tambo).

Mum is not a citizen, but they were so keen to make the election democratic to everyone even a permanent resident. So she could vote!

Mum was very excited as she had left Britain too young to vote there and probably (as proved correct) would never be granted the vote again.

For some reason my folks thought it was great to take Kerry along for the walk to the local school where the ballots would be cast. Mum remembers waiting about 1½ hours in the queue with everyone being very patient and chatting to others.

Kerry and Mum's turn finally came along and into the school hall they went although it was only Mum, of course, who voted.

# HOLLY'S ANTICS

We can't end on a sad note so I will tell you just a few more stories.

I had a good foster child in Holly to pass on some quirky habits.

Holly and Mum used to help an animal charity occasionally by Mum shaking the tin outside a shopping centre. On a Saturday morning they could be seen outside a mall like Rosebank or Hyde Park Corner in Johannesburg's northern suburbs.

Holly always amused the crowd as she darted all over the place while on a lead of course. She was attracted by the glint from Mum's watch for example on the pavement. Mum calls them "Tinkerbells" as Tinkerbell (the fairy in *Peter Pan)* often appeared as a small star.

This activity kept Holly amused for the two to four-hour shift they did. If a dog came shopping with its owner then she had something to say and would bark loudly. Fortunately for Mum, Dad would appear after about 1½ hours to relieve Mum, literally, as by then she needed the loo. He would hold Holly's lead until Mum returned.

Lucky for the animal charity Mum often handed the tin to Denise (with whom she is still friendly) at the end of the morning with no more space in the tin and R50 notes sticking out. That was quite a sum in the mid 1990s!

Mum's enthusiasm for this task dwindled as she was often jostling for a position with beggars also shaking their tin. A former colleague, Soña, out shopping said to Mum: "Oh are you reduced to standing shaking a tin, now?"

Holly would be fascinated by the slide shows Mum and Dad organised to promote the latest destination they had visited, or often repeated one to a new audience on Antarctica. A delicious buffet supper would be served in stages which Mum had prepared herself. The starters and drinks were dished up for the 25 guests, sometimes more, then main course and lots of delicious desserts after the show.

Dad would use a red laser button to point something out on the screen, quite often showing where they had been on the map. Well this small rather round dog, Holly, went nothing short of ballistic pouncing on this beam for all she was worth, to catch it.

She showed her intelligence if she saw it in the big mirror on the adjacent wall by thinking it might have disappeared next door. She would rush down the aisle of the seating in the lounge and into the dining room next door, then back again to find the red dot once more annoying her.

It was hard for the audience to concentrate, amidst their laughter, on the destination they were supposed to be interested in. Fortunately very few managed to doze off!

My folks also had to be careful that the first lot of eats were safe on the dining room table when Humans were out of the room. Springers are always ready to help themselves.

*Holly and Brecon, a new arrival aged one year, who I had taught to swim, cautiously investigate the waves.*

# DAD'S 50th BIRTHDAY OR WUFFDAY

Soon after I had the Big Injection my folks with Brecon and Holly made their way to Arniston on the Cape coast near Cape Agulhas – *the most* southerly cape of Africa – just in case you thought it was the Cape of Good Hope near Cape Town.

I was allowed to watch once I had found myself a reasonably fluffy cloud to curl up on. It is crowded up there when you first arrive with all the best clouds taken. You are allowed to rest at first, after all your labours on earth.

Brecon who was barely one year old thought this 15-hour journey was a huge adventure and sat bolt upright in the back seat of the car looking out of the window which was the nearest thing to doggy television. He took in all sorts of sights and even a strange big bird in a heavily fenced area as they approached the Cape Province. It was an ostrich of course – I knew *that.*

Holly took it in her stride and they had regular stops for piddles/wees and snacks. The major stop was at a butchery in Graaf Reinet which is famous for its tasty Karoo Lamb as the sheep feed off wild rosemary in the local semi arid countryside. My mouth was drooling. There Dad bought a side of lamb to roast on a spit on his big day.

Their destination was a seafront cottage good friends had loaned them. The farming couple would be joining the party along with great friends Hazel and Richard from Cape Town plus Uncle Mike driving down independently. Various other local friends made up the numbers to 13.

On arrival the dogs made themselves at home and Holly was incensed with some slow moving creatures on the front lawn which had a low wall around it.

"What on earth are these," she yapped trying to hurry them along. They were the tortoises which this family had as pets when children and had by now multiplied when left to their own devices as the family grew up.

They all went for long walks along the beach with fascinating rock pools containing odd things to investigate, swimming or jumping around. I must say I was very envious I couldn't be there in the flesh but my illness had got the better of me.

On an open sandy beach they both paddled in the shallows, a bit nervous of the waves. Holly was having none of this and barked furiously that the waves must stop moving that second or she would report them.

The party that night was a howling success – as Dad insisted on serenading as he liked to do with his operatic-trained voice. A dog's singing voice is of course a howl which is why I call it "howling". Lots of tidbits conveniently came the way of the two landlubbers, Holly and Brecon.

They all rested on Sunday with any guests staying over departing after a late breakfast. They all had more walks on the beach and packed up the car for an early start for the return journey, leaving at crack of dawn on Monday at 5.30 a.m.

Fortunately Dad is a good long distance driver – some 1800 kms – and while Mum takes over, he has a good snooze, snoring for all to enjoy. He must have been like us, never truly asleep because if Mum let the cassette tape replay he would sit bolt upright, wide awake, rewind it to the beginning, insert it in its box; change the tape for a new one – occasionally asking Mum if she wanted her "normal" music or to carry on with his endless classical music tapes.

("Normal" for Mum was something from the musicals, or the 1960's pop songs.)

A second later he would be snoring again. It sounds like us dogs; we always have one minuscule part of us awake, just in case.

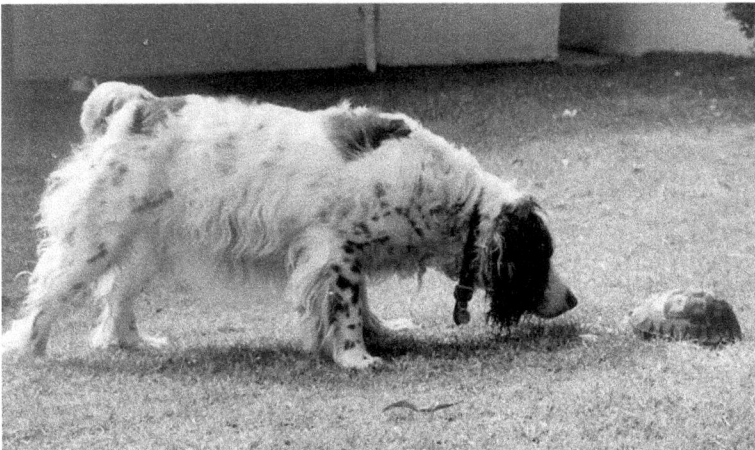

*After I had to cross Rainbow Bridge after my long life Dad had planned a trip to the coast to celebrate his 50th birthday. Here Holly is saying hello to the local tortoise in their friend's garden.*

# AGGRESSIVENESS

Despite my rather eccentric nature (so I am told) I was friendly with everyone. Lay on a party and I'm there, being the star of the show, even outshining my Dad who often felt he must perform his songs when he had a captive audience.

However there is always one lapse. Holly, didn't make pals easily. But this little round short legged dog, adored the rather handsome (if I say so myself) black Alsatian we learned was called Tuffy. He would appear regularly in the Recreation Centre park having hopped over the wall with ease from his house nearby.

Holly really overdid her flirtation, leaping out of the half-open rear window of Mum's car once as we slowed down to park outside the fence surrounding this park. People yelled at Mum who didn't immediately realise what had happened. Fortunately Holly was fine, picked herself up and was off to greet Tuffy.

I really had to put a stop to that, especially on another occasion when I saw him flirting with another lady dog. He would break Holly's heart! Of course he was much bigger than me; but that never stopped me. Fortunately no damage was done to either of us.

Mum carried on the liaison by sending a Christmas card to Tuffy from Holly; she popped it in the letter box on the wall which Tuffy soared over.

A year or two went by and Mum sometimes did the rounds of dropping brochures or had another reason to call in to this travel agency where she was greeted with strange looks and giggles. Eventually the senior consultant, Vera, said "Do you have a dog called Holly?"

Mum, puzzled by such an odd question, agreed this was true. Vera, replied: "Well, Tuffy is *my* dog!

Mum blushed to the roots of her hair being thanked for Tuffy's Christmas card! As this wasn't her agency there was nowhere to hide. The favourite thing Mum did if she didn't want to see a visitor in her own agency was to crouch behind her desk which often had a central empty space in which to hide!

They bumped into each other in the supermarket a couple of times and Mum told her when Holly passed away and heard on another occasion that sadly Tuffy had died too.

The two ladies have recently been re-introduced and meet for coffee and have lots to talk about.

*Holly doted on Tuffy, even to the extent of jumping out of the car window once in the local park. I am not sure I can allow this carry-on.*

# DOGGY VISITORS

We often had other dogs to stay. For some reason (probably Robyn was in season) the ladies went to stay with Lionel but he had to send his males to us: a Collie, called Blue I think, a Labrador as well as another Springer, Glen. A visitor remarked how like me Glen and I were. The penny dropped that he was probably my father. Lionel didn't seem to know who my Dad was and Robyn wasn't telling "tails".

It was chaos in our small garden and I didn't like it one bit. The Collie wanted to herd *me* all over the show.

I am not sure what happened but Dad soon said we couldn't cope with these large dogs and Lionel must make other arrangements.

Another time we had a dachsie to stay who normally lived in a flat in the centre of downtown Johannesburg. He arrived with about three knitted coats on. It was winter but not *that* cold. Dad removed all these coats and the dachsie was in heaven. He rolled on "real grass" and ran around losing weight as he did so as he was rather rotund from lack of exercise.

I relate this to say that I was a social kind of guy; let alone with all the humans they entertained and visitors who dropped in.

# THE REST OF THE GANG . . .

Talking of food, I passed on a good piece of advice to Emily and Nina up in heaven before they were born, once I had done some fast talking to the man on the gate I had to enter after crossing Rainbow Bridge. I insisted I was worthy of coming into heaven. This man with wings said I had upset some of his feathered friends on earth and I shouldn't be there. I said it was in my genes as a hunting dog and a few other remarks to get me admitted. It was worse than any border post my parents have negotiated on their travels. I felt I should have applied for a Visa before leaving earth!

Almost as a joke Mum had seen the advertisement for very expensive Springer pups for sale in the paper and passed it onto Dad as they were now divorced and Dad had by then moved into his new house in Linden a few months earlier.

Emily and her sister Nina arrived as scrawny pups in February after the year that I died. They were flown up from Durban full of ticks and could easily have succumbed to biliary (tick bite fever) to join me back on my cloud.

Emily loved her food and thought she had gone to heaven if she managed to get shut into Dad's rather untidy guest bedroom stacked with boxes, some of which contained the newly baked biscuits Aunt Bridget gave him from her new dog biscuit factory.

These were packed loose in big boxes and sometimes not sealed down. It was easy for a small nose to poke its way in and eat and eat and eat. Then there was a convenient bed to have a nap. She never uttered a sound of complaint that she would like to be rescued.

Eventually Dad would find her but think it was a mistake that Emily had been shut in the room as the wind had probably blown the door shut; so she was treated like a prodigal daughter.

Only later he would find the level of the biscuits had mysteriously diminished . . .

Both Emily and Nina had to live with Mum after Dad died and Em repeated this trick by being stuck in her storeroom sometimes on purpose. This didn't fool Mum one bit! By now Mum had a good stock of Bridget's biscuits in sealed containers but you never knew your luck thought Em.

She had also once found Em inside the tiny corner pantry cupboard in her kitchen at the Parkhurst house. When she copied the same cupboard in the new kitchen in Blairgowrie where she moved after Dad died, she asked the carpenter to fix a lock on this cupboard.

He duly did so and handed Mum the set of keys proud of completing his task saying he had locked the door already to save the contents from intruders.

She looked puzzled and said with a laugh: "No I don't need to remove the keys, thanks; as long as the grocery door is locked; it's to stop the dogs getting inside the cupboard."

# COOPER . . .

. . . aged 14 months, was in kennels awaiting the Big
Injection when Dad heard of his plight. By now he and
Mum were divorced and the only hassles they had was
he insisted on hosting Holly and Brecon for two weeks
at a time while he already had Emily and Nina full time.

Denise (who owned Bouviers) called it "Custardy" as
opposed to Custody. Mum never thought it was in the
least bit funny not to have dogs around *her* house.

Mum agreed immediately to them both adopting
Cooper so she would always have at least one dog at all
times in her house in the future. This lovely large
Springer was rescued in the nick of time. The four
inmates at Dad's were a bit nervous as they'd heard he
was being "done away with" as he was aggressive
fighting their other dog, a Labrador.

Nothing could be further from the truth. While the
four: Emily, Nina, Holly and Brecon and Mum sat in
Dad's garden awaiting his arrival, this huge dog jumped
out slowly from Dad's car, made a big puddle and sub-
missively came towards them with his tail between his
legs.

They soon flocked round him sniffing this strange
creature and he couldn't stop piddling poor chap. He had
been named Cooper so the name stuck. Whether he was

named for a Mini Cooper car or perhaps the famous boxer; we never knew.

Eventually we heard this family living in Dainfern got rid of their Labrador. Their loss was our gain.

Cooper was a much heavier set dog than us, who were all the Working English Springer Spaniels. Cooper must have been the Show variety with his huge drooping, almost Basset Hound sized ears and mournful eyes. His claim to fame was that humans must throw balls constantly especially his favourite soft toy soccer ball at home in the small Parkhurst garden which frequently came to grief. Springers are experts at disembowelling the fluff through the tiniest hole! Possibly someone else assisted hoping the ball games would cease? Springers are keen to rest after their labours during the day.

Mum needed to keep a few in stock. Fortunately Aunt Denise found that a well-known supermarket chain stocked them in their toy section.

Cooper brought a tennis ball when on walks in the park. If he didn't have his ball, he barked, barked and barked some more. Once down at Dad's place in Rosendal, in the Free State, near Lesotho, where you could walk for miles he barked the whole two hours or more on a walk with much more interesting sniffs to entertain the rest of us. He only wanted to chase his ball which had been left back at the house.

Mum had to take him to a therapist to calm him down with a complicated technique known as the Tellington Touch.

Aunt Hertha was asked to tea from next door as a guinea pig in this experiment. Like a small child Cooper would be allowed in the room if he kept quiet, rather a necessity as Mum worked from home and was always consulting with clients about their travel arrangements.

If he barked, out the door he would go. When he stopped he could come in. Bark and he was shut out. After 12 times he finally got the message. This exercise had to be repeated only once or twice more and that problem was solved.

The Tellington Touch involved many other massage techniques and also wrapping his body up in a bandage in a figure of eight. This calmed Cooper down but you couldn't leave it on for too long as he couldn't wee or poo with this wide bandage covering his whole body.

*Sponsor was one of Cooper's pals and went up and down the slide by himself if he felt like it.*

# BEN AND SALLY

After Holly went to Rainbow Bridge, Mum was very sad and while waiting in her supermarket finding out if a product was in stock, she glanced at the local paper. There was an advertisement for two Springers needing good homes.

It wasn't long before Dad was driving her to an animal sanctuary far north of Pretoria with two of the resident Springers as examples to see if they would all get on. It was a strange place in the bush whose focus was to rescue some of the police force's Alsatians. A batch had just been bought on auction that morning so the two ladies had to attend to injecting them with vitamins, giving them water and generally housing them first as most of them were in poor health.

The two dogs who went along got into agonies with nasty minute thorns in their paws – I think known as *duiweltjies* or devil's thorns. As the journey had taken about 1½ hours and while they waited patiently for an hour Dad eventually asked them to please bring the two Springers to introduce them to everyone. More time elapsed as it turned out the younger girl refused to be caught. Who does that remind you of?

Eventually both Ben (then named Big Boy – well really what a silly name), a very handsome six year old spotty black and white guy and his litter mate (that means born of the same parents but from a different litter) Shaggie (again *who* gives a dog *that* name) immediately renamed Sally arrived aged two. She had in fact just had her birthday in the kennels not that anyone took any notice. Sally was almost pure white with a couple of black markings.

So they soon changed their surname to Meintjes and home they came. They went to Mum's home for a couple of weeks for lots of TLC* as Dad was always out working.

She fed them with tidbits, had them checked out at the Vet (both had ear infections); gave them a bath and took them for short walks in the local park, on leads in the early days.

Ben was stressed out with all the homes he had lived in and protecting Sally so immediately attached himself to Dad and mostly lived with him. Sally was immediately "at home" and adored Dad's big garden and ran and ran and ran some more. She only stopped to slurp some water from her bowl and off she went again for another circuit. They had spent a year in the previous lady's parents' town house garden (which are postage stamp size) and had never once been taken for walks in Durban in case they ran away! Her parents were moving to a flat on the South Coast so they could no longer cope with these dogs.

Mum heard all this history from a phone call on the way home from the previous owner. This lady Cheryl had to give up her job, her home and her dogs all at once. Her fiancé had broken off their engagement, and, as he

* TLC Tender Loving Care

103

was the boss of the firm she worked for, saw fit to fire her as well.

This kennel, for a fee, would not put the dogs down and would try to rehome them. Cheryl had already paid their board and lodging but they were not averse to asking for a donation from Mum and Dad too.

Cheryl came to visit Mum a few times from Durban so she could see her dogs again; something Dad frowned upon as Ben and Sally must now realise the houses in Parkhurst and Linden were now their "forever" homes.

Although Cheryl was given another Springer, a girl called Brandy, by a new boyfriend in Umhlanga, and she already had a Yorkie in her flat in Durban; while of "unsound" mind she committed suicide by hanging which shocked Mum for a long time. They had often chatted on her mobile, usually while Mum was out walking all of them in the vast Emmarentia park, on a Saturday morning.

*The next bossy-paw after me: the rescued PaWsi, who advertised herself as a Springer so she joined the family very nervous at 6 months.*

# PRESENT DOGS HOLDING THE BONE

## (Baton Says Mum)

Mum had seven (yes 7 dogs) when Dad died so suddenly on 4 April 2013. We think it was a heart attack following a robbery early that morning. I suddenly had to assemble: Robyn, Kerry, Holly, Brecon and recent arrival Sally as well as get myself into a presentable state to meet him at Rainbow Bridge. What a rush that day was!

This was nothing to what faced the other dogs and Mum. She had recently broken her leg in two places in Emmarentia park during a walk. Fortunately she was with the new pup, Bramble and his Dad, Djuma, owned by "Granny" Jeannine. However, one of these black and white Springers thumped into Mum's leg while her back was turned, so perhaps if it wasn't one year old Bramble it would have been the other Springer, his Dad.

Jeannine got permission to drive her 4x4 car into the park to pick up Cooper (who naturally still expected Mum to throw the ball while she was sitting tearfully on the ground), Pawsi, Bramble and her own three dogs. Mum phoned Dad on her mobile saying this calamity had happened.

Dad had been due to arrive with the rest: Ben, Hugo (Bramble's brother), Nina and Emily.

He said the most amazing thing: "OK, I'll be along and bring the others for a walk first." Mum was lost for words saying she thought she should be taken to hospital, possibly with a broken ankle. Already passers-by were advocating she didn't touch a drop from her water bottle, which she always carried with her, in case of an operation later that day.

To cut a long story short, it turned out Mum had to have an operation to set her leg that Sunday evening. For the next few weeks Dad helped shop for groceries and medicines for her and called round at her house almost daily. This no doubt added to his stress levels in trying to get some work done.

On 4 April she heard from Dad on his mobile who was asking how she was that day. Then he nearly dropped the cordless phone. He realised his mobile had been stolen in a robbery earlier that day and his office at the back of the house had been ransacked with the laptop and camera he needed for work gone. He would stay at home awaiting the police to take fingerprints.

When she could not reach him on the landline that afternoon for an hour or two with its busy signal, she had a premonition something was *very* amiss. Mum was only mobile in a wheelchair or on crutches. She could not drive over to find out what had happened.

She asked her maid Dolly to leave early that afternoon to hurry home to Linden as she stayed on Dad's premises but Dolly first had to take in the laundry drying in the garden down some steps (so Mum couldn't help) and was then dependent on catching an African taxi to reach Linden, a suburb only five minutes' drive by car.

She found Chris collapsed in the bathroom, phoned Mum who immediately called an ambulance. She finally got a lift there when one of cottage tenants had returned home early.

The Ambulance men declared him dead. Then followed a horrendous evening waiting for the police and mortuary people who eventually came to the house.

Apart from the horrendous weeks that followed Mum realised she would have to move house from Parkhurst, once Dad's dilapidated house was sold as she had *seven* dogs to look after.

For now they would commute between the two residences. Fortunately the building society who was still owed money on Dad's mortgage provided a wonderful guard, John, who was on duty 24/7. Dolly still cleaned Dad's house on the same days and slept there so they did have company as well as John.

Mum usually had all the dogs at weekends where they were spoilt rotten with walks (usually all seven at once), given treats, brushed and bathed, if necessary, and then rotated them around as to who lived where during the next week. She still visited Dad's house several times in the week and took them for walks.

# WHERE & WHEN DID PAWSI, HUGO

# AND BRAMBLE ARRIVE?

I have forgotten to say how Pawsi and the boys joined the family. Pawsi is a "not quite Springer" but we don't say that to her face. Denise (of Bouvier fame) had a colleague in her dog training class who had a Springer (called Charlie). This lady happened to look at a Spaniel Rescue website that week in September 2008, and there, advertised was a Springer Spaniel in Boksburg. This is a satellite mining town about 30 kms east of Johannesburg.

Once Mum heard about an unwanted Springer needing a good home (but nothing about "for sale") she just happened to be playing in a croquet tournament in the neighbouring town of Benoni that Sunday.

Denise offered to visit the croquet club at the end of the day and Mum would follow in her car, courtesy of Denise's GPS to the house in Boksburg as Mum was totally unfamiliar with these areas. They finally arrived to find an almost black Spaniel/cross Border Collie.

"Mmm," said Mum undecided. She was not a Springer. While Patty, as she was called, seemed very lively and played with a neighbour's Labrador she was apparently no longer wanted because (and they felt they were spun a yarn) about a sick child in hospital so Patty stayed by herself all day and night in the back garden; had never been for a walk unless she (wisely I say) escaped out of the front gate.

She wore a pink collar far too tight for her which Denise immediately loosened. They needed to get going as it was getting late and Mum had another croquet player, Jessie, suffering from a bad cold as a passenger. Denise needed to return home to her dogs too.

Finally Mum said she would take her. "But," said the owner "R500" please. "Good Heavens, people are usually happy to find a good home for their dog," said Mum. "I'll have to spay her soon which will cost a lot," as Patty was apparently around six months old.

"No she cost me over R2000," was the reply. Mum had R200 in her purse so handed that over and promised to do a bank transfer for the rest when she got home.

As Mum carried Patti to the car, the owner followed her and insisted on undoing the pink collar Patti wore as a souvenir. En route home Patty sniffed lovely smells of the other dogs on the blanket on the back seat while the now previous owner kept phoning on her mobile to ask if Mum had made the extra payment yet. She even made Mum promise to stay in touch.

Needless to say Mum changed Patty to Patty-Paws immediately. Then just Pawsi sprung to mind; we dogs always let you know what we would like to be called.

Mum had her checked out at the Vet, who wouldn't believe she wasn't a lot older than six months. Teeth apparently give away your age whether you are dog or human and Pawsi's teeth were brown.

Mum got hold of the breeder via the vet where Pawsi was first vaccinated. She proved she really was six months old. They invited Pawsi's first mum, a lovely lady, to visit Mum once with Java, Pawsi's mother. Java was a Roan Cocker Spaniel. With her black and white markings, but smaller than us, she can at first glance, easily be mistaken for a Springer.

However Pawsi also had a white splash down her front and a long bushy tail, very definitely Border Collie lineage.

Breeder, Leilanie, said a Collie could never be the father as Java lived behind high walls and would never misbehave! It remains a mystery to this day unless Pawsi inherited genes of a "throwback" from her parents.

Pawsi was now Mum's responsibility* and lived at home with Mum, who was travelling the next week to the coast of KwaZulu Natal. The house sitting arrangement was that Dad would normally look after Mum's dogs while she was away. So Pawsi was duly dropped on a Saturday morning while Dad was out shopping.

While Mum had long since left on her trip there were frantic calls on her mobile from Dad: "This dog has crept under my 4x4 and won't come out!"

Oops! She was scared stiff of men. Dad has always loved dogs and either hunger or his comforting noises eventually drew her out from her hiding place and she never looked back; she adored her new Dad; just

---

* Other dogs they adopted, meant they would share expenses of food and vet bills regardless of whose house they lived in; while Pawsi was totally Mum's dog for all costs.

occasionally appearing a bit nervous for a while when another of the human male species, visited.

I leave you to draw your own conclusions of mistreatment and maybe money laundering with dogs. Leilanie never sold the pup for anything like R2000. Pawsi *was only* six months old and bit of doggy toothpaste soon made her teeth "Maclean's clean".

Thank heavens this effort of cleaning dog's teeth wasn't invented in *my* day! Just give me a bone!

*Gathering in Jo's garden of some of the pups with parents Lily (brown and white) and Djuma (black and white) sitting next to their 'grannies' Kelly and Jeannine.*

# LAST BUT NOT LEAST:

## PUPS BRAMBLE AND HUGO

Mum is not very gregarious until it comes to talking to a Springer Spaniel, whose name she generally remembers, and then speaks to the owner, who's name she promptly forgets.

This was how she met Lily, a liver and white lady Springer, in the Recreation Centre in Parkhurst. She was owned by a Canadian couple. Her mum, Kelly, said she would soon find her a mate before their contract expired the following year and the family returned to Canada.

Time went by and suddenly there was a phone call "Come and see the Pups."

Lily and Djuma (a black and white Springer) whose Mums had met in the Linden cycle shop had *eleven*, I kid you not, pups were born and all thrived. Lily was quite a small Springer but she had great help from all her owner's family helping feed some pups with a bottle. Kelly slept in the same room as the pups to make sure all went well. Breeders and dog trainers who ultimately came to buy a pup were amazed how healthy the whole litter were.

There were six black and white pups and five liver and white with male and female in each colour to choose from.

When they were 10 days old Mum and Dad visited. Should they buy a pup was the decision? Surely not, they had just buried poor Sally who had turned blind at a young age and had suffered for several months from a weird incurable gastric problem. Remaining in the family were almost blind brother Ben – which shows breeders should check the genes of the parents before breeding twice – fairly elderly sisters Nina and Emily; Cooper, and of course PaWsi who had now taken charge! (She likes that spelling!)

They would share a male pup. No, they would have a male pup each! They often went to visit before a small black and white pup decided he would zoom over to Mum as fast as his legs would carry him in the outside puppy playpen decorated with a miniature tyre suspended on a rope. This was decorated with other obstacles just like a children's playground.

Dad also chose a black and white pup.

Once when they visited, the pups had been to visit their Dad, Djuma, in Emmarentia for the first time.

Kelly had colour co-ordinated the puppies for travelling there and back into two laundry baskets. Luckily as the hatch at the back of the car was opened Dad had his camera ready and there they were already trying to wriggle out. Kelly and her two boys, plus my Humans trying to assist, helped carry the basket heaving with puppies inside the property and quickly tipped them into their playpen before any mishaps.

Dad chose Hugo, shortened to Hugz, who often visited Mum as Dad was out so much and of course he needed his three meals a day at that age. Mum didn't name Bramble for a while, but it suddenly came to her in a dream (I *told* you dogs tell you their names) and "Granny" Kelly said she thought that was the best named pup in the whole litter!

They both fitted into a small basket looking as if "butter wouldn't melt in their mouths." Time passed and soon it was time for dog school.

Of course these pups hadn't seen each other for a week sometimes so there was plenty of "gossip" to catch up on when they did meet. The trainer was surprised that they were so impossible before class started as Mum and Dad had signed up as a married couple for cheaper rates.

There were large classes so a lot of waiting for your turn was experienced, something no Springer likes. They would quite easily have volunteered ten times to do the exercise required like "Retrieve" than wait and wait. Hugo was particularly good at this one but Bramble saw it as an excuse to come back via a detour visiting the other classes.

They liked it when first one parent had to go and hide behind a tree and call their pup. Sometimes Bramble thought it necessary to deviate en route, like have a wee, which wasn't considered good manners.

They did graduate to a higher class but soon after the end of year loomed in November and they were told to come for a "very easy test" the next Saturday after which would be a celebratory tea. When the day arrived suddenly both human and pup were expected to perform tests they had never done even once! How can a dog walk to heel without a lead if he or she has never done so before? Another example was to have the dog off the lead and expect it to sit, throw the ball and when it landed only then were they allowed to retrieve.

You try doing that with either of these two – it spelled **Disaster.**

The other participants weren't very amused either and before the exam time was up Mum and Dad slunk off with their charges. It was also very tiring for them as Dad especially liked his Saturday afternoon nap and in the heat of summer two hours of holding, running, weaving in and out of other owners with their dogs (every one of whom these two wanted to stop and chat!) proved extremely tiring. After class the dogs would immediately snooze in the back seat of their respective parents' cars while they were chauffeur-driven home.

One afternoon Dad couldn't be there so Mum took both dogs thinking the trainer would help with Hugo's turn. No way! Fortunately a visitor watching held him while Mum did the exercise with Bramble. Then swop dogs and repeat with Hugo. Mum felt she had run a relay race by the end of the afternoon!

When Dad died these two active boys could have benefited from more classes but it would have meant attending on alternate Saturdays and who was going to remember that much if you only attended once a fortnight? After all there was now only Mum as a handler.

She was brave enough to do a walk with all seven sometimes driving about 30 minutes to Huddle Park to meet up with Grace for a dog's birthday party. But more often Jo would walk them in twos and threes to different parks in one day, making sure blind Ben could at least enjoy fresh air and dig up a fresh mole hill or two.

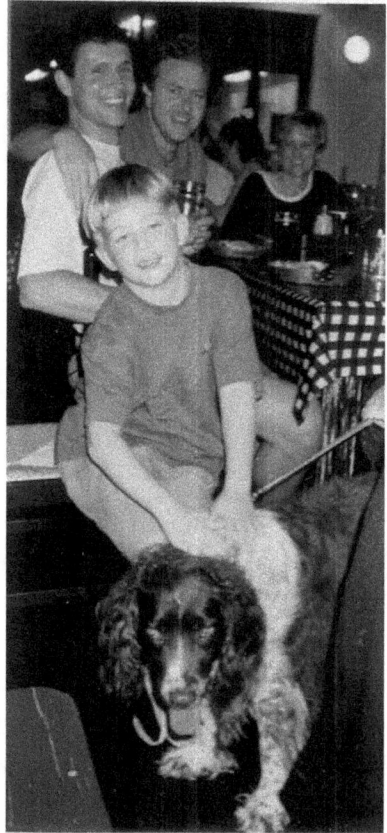

*One of my last outings to meet my good friend Uncle Gavin with his son James on his son's first visit to South Africa. I was permitted entry to the restaurant which was when pets were banned.*

# POST SCRIPT

I have only just remembered to tell you how I first met Gavin. He was a real outdoors person and if I may say, I think I followed a little in his footsteps. I had heard Dad saying to Mum that Gavin had walked the length of the South African coastline. Yes really, from the border with Mocambique to the border with Namibia, although it was then called South West Africa. He never made a big deal of it, nor got sponsorship, or wrote a book like people would these days.

He wanted to show my parents how he had mastered archery and Dad must show him which gun he should buy for his next adventure as security. So off we set one Saturday in Dad's new 4x4 *bakkie.* We were going to the Northern Transvaal to Galpin's farm but would be camping. Dad had fitted a mattress into the back of this *bakkie* with a cover over the back. I was going to sleep in the passenger/driving compartment in front.

Mum had been busy borrowing a sewing machine to run up some curtains to darken the back section as she couldn't stand moonlight or daylight waking her up.

Gavin arrived under his own steam.

That afternoon we all went for a walk. I should explain that this farm was next to a well-known bird reserve so there was plenty for me to do. I was still a very young chap and had never been in the bush before so was a

117

teeny bit scared, that is well behaved in human eyes. After all I had been trained by Lionel hadn't I? I didn't need to be on a lead.

Everyone seemed to think I was being so good. They didn't notice me for a second or two as something caught my attention.

The next time Dad looked down there was no me there. So Dad called and called. Mum called and called. Gavin whistled. No me in sight. Dad yelled and yelled. Still no me.

Apparently this went on for an hour or more. Gavin had to keep a straight face and it led him, as a superb illustrator, drawing a special cartoon of Dad bursting his lungs out calling for me. They really thought I was lost for good.

Gavin said I would turn up eventually as the whole place was fenced. They returned to camp with Mum very worried. The men started a fire for an early *braai* before the sun went down in the cool autumn weather. With the smell of delicious *boerewors* – the local farmers' South African sausage – and a steak on the grid I eventually turned up full of black jacks. As you have read these are nasty spikes and by winter they are everywhere in the bush. The seed heads make coats like ours stick up like pin cushions.

They saved the day as no one could get near me to wring me by the scruff of my neck without hurting their hands on these spikes. As I said before, physical abuse was dished out frequently, in my case, in that bygone era.

I slept like a log that night in the comfy front seats. Mum was really proud of me as I was not potty trained but didn't mess until Mum scrambled out of the back of the truck after a sleepless night. In the small compartment at the back next to Dad who took XX large size in clothing it was very squashed. Perhaps we should have swapped places? It was a "state secret" what Dad weighed. Mum never *ever* did find out!

Gavin left South Africa not long after to marry his Swiss girlfriend he had met here. Her father was the Swiss Consul and when his posting here was over, the family returned to Switzerland; their daughter Danny still in her teens, went with them. Gavin flew his two beloved Airedale dogs over as best men for his wedding. He had no other family at the ceremony.

Dad used his Nissan *bakkie* to gain height for better game viewing in many a game reserve or to sleep in on a hunting expedition with one of us. I only recall one further time Mum and Dad tried to sleep in it. They were on the Natal north coast wanting to visit some of the game reserves like Mkuze. They did have accommodation available but as there was a drought all the visitors were banned from sleeping over.

"Why?" asked Dad, "We have our own supply of water."

There was nothing for it but to turn around and seek another place to stay. Nearby was the Ghost Mountain Inn. Dad asked if they could park there as they had everything they needed to eat so they didn't need to come inside except to use the ablutions. The rather surprised manager agreed for a small fee.

Mum has to have water to drink in the night. By then she had acquired an ex-Chinese army round metal water bottle; probably brought back from Dad leading a trip to China with some of the first ever South African tourists in 1990. He was always keen to travel to a new country once the visa regulations changed, and they were rapidly changing as the politics changed and South Africans were welcomed almost everywhere with open arms.

There was nowhere to put a glass of water, of course, in this confined part of the *bakkie*, so why not rest this metal bottle on the bull bar over their heads?

That evening Dad had gone to sleep as Mum tossed and turned. After a sip of water she replaced the bottle on the bar. A few seconds later Dad yelped. It had fallen on his head. The result was a black eye for him.

This, of course, was later jokingly blamed on Mum socking him one in an argument.

For some reason my family became known as The Blott family. Something to do with the frequently heard phrase around our house: "Merlyn has blotted his copy-book – *again!*"

However my name did have its uses.

There came a time when Mum was running her own IATA approved larger travel business. Anne Marie now helped by organising weekends away for the clients. It was known as The Lourie Club because at that time the Grey Lourie bird was only found in the bush and not seen in Johannesburg. As they started to migrate into in town that name became redundant, as did the club.

The National Parks Board had only just set up trail camps set in remote parts of The Kruger National Park. They were for six people for three or four night trips.

They were highly sought after and awarded by a lottery type method. You were taken by an armed ranger on walks in the early morning and from mid-afternoon; sometimes he would drive you so it became part game drive/part walk. The small staff at the rustic camp would cook delicious meals around the open fire before you slept in the basic huts. Ablutions were communal nearby.

Mum's business had some luck with getting trails and selling them onto her clients with a booking fee attached, which since they were so hard to obtain, people were happy to pay.

One day their slot on the Olifants Trail was not fully booked so Anne Marie told the Parks Board there were still two spaces. A few days later Mum took the call from a man who wanted to know if he and his girlfriend could come on Mr D Blott's trail. She was totally bemused but handed the phone to Anne Marie who calmly said they could take the two spare places.

"What a shame Mr D Blott can't come," he said.

"Yes it is, his wife wouldn't let him travel," she replied.

Anne Marie had thought to apply in the name of Mr D (for Dog) Blott as the name of the party leader!

Anne Marie and Mum went on this trail – a lovely spot away from all the main camps with the Olifants River running over pretty smooth potholes as you find in nearby Bourke's Luck Potholes. At the last evening's *braai* after a glass of two of wine, they and this couple lingered by the camp fire. They again enquired after Mr Blott's family and how kind it was of him to give up these two places.

This time the ladies burst out laughing so Anne Marie had to explain that Mr Blott was Jo's Springer Spaniel and she had made up the story about my wife, presumably Robyn, not allowing me to travel. Fortunately all of them had a good laugh about the situation.

Dogs are sadly not allowed in the National Parks as I would have loved to have gone to the bush once more.

So all resident dogs are now still called The Blotties by Charlotte who sends them her love, now and again, from their McBrides game lodge in Zambia.

*The litter's 1st birthday held at 'granny' Jeannine's house. Their Dad, Djuma, in the background. Jo holds onto Bramble and Hugo. And so the line continues as they are the 12th & 13th in the Meintjes family.*

# PPS (POST POSTSCRIPT)

As Mum assists me with my autobiography only PaWsi, Bramble and Hugo remain in the family. They are pampered like never before. When she finishes a meal she walks round to where they are lounging on a sofa or in an armchair to offer them a lick of leftover on the plate. This is to say nothing of their annual wuffday parties maybe to be told at another time.

I hope I have helped explain what a unique and strange breed of dog we are with my eccentricity in particular. I suppose it is not surprising that there are several Spaniel rescue societies to help re-home dogs that at first don't fit in with their first home.

Mum and Dad, just prior to his death, helped re-home Sammy, one of the 11 pups, who had not ended up at his "forever" home. Discussions were held on the croquet lawn at the smart Jo'burg Country Club when Dad heard that John was about to put down his beloved husky and had once owned a Springer.

However the owner was incensed that anyone had heard him say he wanted to get rid of Samuel whom Mum often met in the local park and whom he called "useless" as Sammy didn't want to chase a ball. Eventually matters were arranged with another of the pup's owners pretending she knew John. Laurie and John had to meet this guy pretending to know each other where Sammy finally was handed over to his "forever" home.

All dogs need "forever" homes but sadly there are far too many animal rescue centres overflowing with animals, many of whom have to be euthanized as they don't have endless funds for food, kennels and other supplies. Mum helps out with donations whenever she can and will do so with a percentage from the sale of this book.

Of course owners die but can't family members help out? Or if the elderly person is going into a retirement home they must choose somewhere they are allowed to take their pets until their time comes. It is now a fact that even if strange dogs visit patients of all ages in hospital they receive much comfort from their visit.

We won't even discuss the horrific cruelty of throwing a pet out of a car on a highway because the owner won't organise a kennel while they are away. I would like to see the tables turned on them in their next life and see how they like it.

However long you are away from home we are always pleased to see you and will never tell you off. I would like to say we are the ideal companions.

# THE MEINTJES' SPRINGER SPANIEL TIME LINE

| Name | Colour | Sex | Birth | Adopted | Died |
|------|--------|-----|-------|---------|------|
| Merlyn | L&W | M | 19.11.1983 | Puppy 8.1.1984 | 5.5.2000 |
| Robyn | L&W | F | 1.8.1980 | 1.5.1985 | 9.9.1993 |
| Kerry | L&W | F | 17.2.1986 | daughter Merlyn/Robyn | 11.7.1999 |
| Holly | L&W | F | Oct 1992 | SPCA 28.12.1992 | 16.10.2005 |
| Brecon | L&W | M | 9.4.1999 | Puppy 12.6.1999 | 16.10.2007 |
| Emily | L&W | F | 8.12.2000 | Puppy | 18.12.2014 |
| Nina | L&W | F | 8.12.2000 | Puppy | 13.11.2015 |
| Cooper | L&W | M | 19.1.2002 | 10.3.2003 | 3.5.2014 |
| Benedict | B&W | M | 22.11.2000 | 27.5.2006 | 18.12.2014 |
| Sally | B&W | F | 22.5.2004 | 27.5.2006 | 7.3.2012 |
| Pawsi | Spaniel/ Collie | F | 14.3.2008 | 7.9.2008 | |
| Bramble | B&W | M | 6.2.2012 | Puppy 31.3.2012 | |
| Hugo | B&W | M | 6.2.2012 | Puppy 31.3.2012 | |
| **Master** | | | | | |
| Chris Meintjes | | M | 29.5.1950 | | 4.4.2013 |
| **Mistress** | | | | | |
| Jo Meintjes | | F | 29.7.1948 | | |

www.ingramcontent.com/pod-product-compliance
Lightning Source LLC
Chambersburg PA
CBHW071835090426
42737CB00012B/2246